Becoming a Lean Library

CHANDOS
INFORMATION PROFESSIONAL SERIES

Series Editor: Ruth Rikowski
(email: Rikowskigr@aol.com)

Chandos' new series of books is aimed at the busy information professional. They have been specially commissioned to provide the reader with an authoritative view of current thinking. They are designed to provide easy-to-read and (most importantly) practical coverage of topics that are of interest to librarians and other information professionals. If you would like a full listing of current and forthcoming titles, please visit www.chandospublishing.com.

New authors: we are always pleased to receive ideas for new titles; if you would like to write a book for Chandos, please contact Dr Glyn Jones on g.jones.2@elsevier.com or telephone +44 (0) 1865 843000.

Becoming a Lean Library

Lessons from the World of Technology Start-ups

JEREMY NELSON

ELSEVIER

Amsterdam • Boston • Cambridge • Heidelberg
London • New York • Oxford • Paris • San Diego
San Francisco • Singapore • Sydney • Tokyo
Chandos Publishing is an imprint of Elsevier

CHANDOS
PUBLISHING

Chandos Publishing is an imprint of Elsevier
225 Wyman Street, Waltham, MA 02451, USA
Langford Lane, Kidlington, OX5 1GB, UK

ISBN: 978-1-84334-779-8 (print)
ISBN: 978-1-78063-460-9 (online)

British Library Cataloguing-in-Publication Data
A catalogue record for this book is available from the British Library

Library of Congress Cataloging-in-Publication Data
A catalog record for this book is available from the Library of Congress

For information on all Chandos Publishing publications
visit our website at http://store.elsevier.com/

Working together
to grow libraries in
developing countries

www.elsevier.com • www.bookaid.org

DEDICATION

To my grandmother Ethel Plummer Nelson and to all knowledge seekers everywhere.

CONTENTS

Please see the Companion Website for the chance to earn two Openbadges:
http://www.becomingleanlibrary.com.

ABOUT THE AUTHOR

Jeremy Nelson is the Metadata and Systems Librarian at Colorado College. He has worked as a librarian at two other academic institutions. Before becoming a librarian, Nelson worked as project manager and programmer at various software companies in the financial services, scientific computing, and educational fields. Nelson has published and presented at numerous regional, national, and international conferences regarding his research in designing and developing open-source bibliographic and semantic Web technologies, with a focus on extending the Catalog Pull Platform. Nelson is graduate of Knox College and the Graduate School of Library and Information Science at the University of Illinois.

FOREWORD

In her 2006 short story, "In the House of Seven Librarians," Ellen Klages imbues a small Carnegie Library with magical abilities including providing a group of isolated librarians with books, supplies, and treats, as well as adjusting its stacks and shelves based on the needs of a young girl, the protagonist of the story. The nostalgia for a public place that nevertheless caters to the intellectual life of the individual person is a common sentiment among library patrons of a certain age, but is a vision that is difficult to realize in the age of declining financial support coupled with increasing demands for technology-focused resources and services.

Inspired by the Lean Startup and Lean Manufacturing movements for existing and new organizations, *Becoming a Lean Library* provides both an explanation and practical tips for the design, management, and delivery of library technology and services based on the concept of "pulling" requirements and needs directly from patrons instead of trying to predict what the patrons will want in some indeterminate future and building the technology and services based on those predictions.

This book attempts to articulate an ongoing process for library technology and services improvement, not a final destination. You're encouraged to join the community of readers and earn your Learner Open Badge at the book's website, http://becomingleanlibrary.com/. As you become more familiar with the theories behind lean manufacturing, lean startups, and pull platforms, and how they can be applied to your next library technology project, you're encouraged to express your ideas about what works and what we needs to improve by earning your Lean Library Leadership badge. This edition of *Becoming a Lean Library* is just the first minimum viable product in an extended build—measure—learn cycle; I believe we still have a lot to learn as we improve our service to our patrons through creating learning environments of knowledge creation in our libraries and for our modern communities.

Jeremy Nelson
Colorado Springs, Colorado
17 October, 2015

CHAPTER 1

Introduction

1.1 PURPOSE

We're no longer limited simply to the 150 people we can maintain physical-world relationships with, to the books on the shelf across the room, or even those at the local library.

Hagel III, Brown, and Davison (2010, p. 71)

The first, and perhaps most obvious but hardest way to approach creating services that are local, personal, relevant and authentic is to start by designing the experience around the needs, expectations and behaviors of the people its intended for.

Nick Poole (2014)

Libraries, like many institutions today, face an existential crisis about their core identity and function in the networked and screen-dominated world (Sternstein, 2005; Williams, 2011). Never before have libraries faced such fundamental questions about their continued existence and relevance. Anecdotally, I am often asked variants of the question, "Are libraries still needed today?" when individuals I encounter find out I am a librarian.

Libraries still enjoy a trusted reputation as a source for books, magazines, journals, and research help that are available to anyone who walks through their doors. The challenge for library leadership and staff is keeping the library relevant in this age of rapid and significant technology changes. Libraries—as well as a large number of companies—can no longer depend on the "tried and true" methods and techniques of years past that are rapidly becoming obsolete as organizations attempt to keep and grow their customer base. Library patrons are able to immediately answer their questions through a simple Web search, a task that just a generation ago would have required either a visit or phone call to the library.

In a 2011 presentation to the National and State Librarians of Australasia, provocatively titled, "Libraries: Where It All Went Wrong," Nate Torkington (2011) listed five areas where libraries have failed to change as organizations as their collections, as he puts it, change from "atoms to bits." Physical books, periodicals, and audio and video collections, while still actively used and cherished by the majority of library patrons, are being both augmented and superseded by the adoption of digital formats for journals and books.

Becoming a Lean Library
ISBN 978-1-84334-779-8

Electronic formats have very different properties than their physical counterparts. Torkington listed these differences as follows:

- Copying of electronic text is vastly easier and cheaper than copying physical text contained in periodicals or books.
- Patrons expect access to their library's collections through networked devices and Web browsers, especially for material that has already been digitized.
- Libraries are no longer an exclusive source for information. The Internet increases knowledge creation and distribution, requiring libraries to seek out new roles in capturing and preserving the digital heritage for future generations.
- Because information online is so easy to create, copy, and distribute, librarians must educate their patrons on information literacy and research skills to cope with the important task of discriminating the useful and the good from the distracting and the poorly researched.
- Finally, librarians need to take advantage of how the Internet is able to connect them with other libraries while accepting that their collections are no longer "theirs" but should be shared with their patrons and their wider communities.

In an environment of corporate multibillion-dollar search tools coupled with increasingly powerful networked mobile devices, how can libraries respond effectively in this new landscape of information? Responding requires major shifts in library operations, collections, and services. Libraries need to go from being passive repositories of physical information artifacts to curating, publishing, and enabling through physical spaces their communities' creative works no matter what the format or media carrier. By encouraging engagement of readers and creators in their communities, libraries expand the meaning and scope of what they collect, proving their utility and necessity in the modern world.

This book explores ways and methods a library can repurpose or reengage staff for this new era of information abundance. By developing management structures and organizational philosophies that focuses on patrons using a library, these lean principles offer ways a library can increase better effects and outcomes than ever before. More than a specific location with an inventory of material for checkout by patrons, the twenty-first-century library is a fluid and exciting space, offering physical space and online services for creative expression by local and global patrons. Libraries that conclusively create compelling narratives, supported by detailed and accurate metrics, thrive by increasing patron opportunities as they interact with the library's collections and with each other throughout their wider communities. Backed by extensive and accurate metrics, patron communities recognize a library's active stewardship of their creative outcomes and artifacts for benefits now and for use by future generations.

How libraries encourage and promote these new narratives hinges on the intersections between services, technology, and people. Delivering complex technology services to meet the demands of their patrons is an increasingly important responsibility for library staff, midlevel managers, and directors. Library leaders depend on the smooth operation of complex technology stacks that run locally at their institution, run entirely through a cloud provider, or, more commonly, a hybrid approach of the two. Libraries must be able to enhance the value of their collections through increased usage and preservation of unique artifacts, while also offering to their patrons more and varied educational services. Regardless of the hosting model of their integrated library system (ILS) and/or digital repository systems, library technology consumes a large portion of a library's budget.

By asking questions and demanding more from library technology partners—be they library system vendors, open-source communities, or other libraries—memory institutions can structure their technologies to better serve and respond to changes within the library. The societal changes occurring in the broader culture that are driven by the changes brought on by networking cheap devices, moving toward a world of ubiquitous computing, requires that libraries shift, adjust, and adapt to these waves of change.

1.2 LANGUAGE AND ORGANIZATION OF THE BOOK

In this book, the term "patron" is used when discussing the primary external constituents of the library. As Aaron Schmidt (2013) commented in a blog post titled, "Focus on People, Not Tools," libraries debate what to call the individuals who enter the library: patrons, participants, members, and now users; the last term is preferred when discussing an individual's use of technologies. Taking Schmidt's larger point, libraries should stop focusing so much on specific technologies. This limits the needed perspective by libraries of the larger impacts of technology by instead examining the long-term consequences and outcomes in the library's relationship to the people it serves. When referring to and discussing library technology that affects everyone, including the library's patrons, librarians, and staff, this book deliberately uses the more general term "user" to indicate this larger scope.

Concepts and terminology common in the lean startup and lean manufacturing industries, introduced in the *Becoming a Lean Library's* early chapters, are also defined in the book's glossary. While libraries' roles and purposes are different from those of for-profit technology startups and established manufacturing companies, libraries benefit from the application of lean principles in structuring their operations and building new services and resources. As libraries strive to serve the changing needs and expectations of patrons and staff while under static, declining, or marginally improving budgetary environments, they must optimize staff's talents and strengths through redundant and responsive library technology for their service communities. By reducing barriers and maximizing the effectiveness of existing operations, libraries can stretch their resources and people through operational and philosophical changes that are driven by capturing and responding to changes in user behavior.

In many chapters a case study is provided that uses examples from my design, development, and implementation of a *catalog pull platform* to explain the chapter's main topics while providing practical lessons for helping the library.

1.3 CATALOG PULL PLATFORM

In their book *The Power of Pull* (2010), John Hagel III and John Seely Brown explain the characteristics and use of a what they call a "pull platform." Unlike traditional enterprise software, the designers and developers of pull platforms do not "push" a set of features that the vendor has built and developed around a product, but instead offer participants tools and connections to build emergent solutions based on their needs and requirements.

Another feature of pull platforms is that they are modular in their design, with minimal coupling with or dependencies on other modules in the platform (Hagel III et al., 2010, p. 76). This feature of loose coupling means that participants discover novel uses of and remix the functionality of the platform while also finding solutions for their problems and issues as they occur. A pull platform does not try to anticipate and address all of the potential issues up front, but instead provides well-documented and flexible interfaces and resources that participants can assemble and test to solve problems as they occur and emerge from use.

Because the components of pull platforms are loosely coupled with each other, specific modules can be enhanced more often with much less interaction effects with other components in the platform. A pull platform initially starts being designed for a specific need, but the platform itself does not assume that the needs and requirements of its participants are known ahead of time (Hagel III et al., 2010, p. 76).

With traditional push software, creative use and "nonstandard" usage, while not explicitly discouraged by vendors, were not usually promoted through official channels or in the vendor's documentation. This is changing as commercial vendors of library systems open up their systems for use and remixing (Breeding, 2014). There are encouraging signs that library vendors are starting to open up their ILS and their library services platforms with application programming interfaces (APIs) for customer use. However, vendors prefer and market their system's "official" user interfaces for library staff and patrons, which are often complex, to support their software's services and functionality.

By contrast, pull platforms actively encourage diversity by connecting diverse viewpoints to solve problems in a distributed and decentralized manner. Innovations and novel uses of the pull platform are celebrated with those innovations distributed through the networks of participants involved in the platform. The technology focus is shifting from trying to push out new upgrades and new versions to one where the pull platform promotes the customization and combination of modules so that participants can quickly solve immediate local problems.

The book's case studies highlight an open-source platform, called the "Catalog Pull Platform," which I developed for use by Tutt Library, Colorado College's academic library; the Colorado Alliance of Research Libraries; and the Library of Congress. The case studies illustrate how libraries use a modern pull platform in their operations. The Catalog Pull Platform is an open-source platform comprising HTML5 Web applications that interact with multiple library systems, including commercial and open-source ILSs, open-source digital repositories, and a new rich semantic server for bibliographic and operational data, called a semantic server. The semantic server interoperates with the semantic Web through a representational state transfer API to Redis, a NoSQL ("no" structured query language) technology widely used in commercial Web operations, and Fedora Commons, one of the most popular open-source digital repository software. The semantic server also includes representational state transfer API interfaces to Elastic Search's Lucene full-text search engine.

A new library catalog for Colorado College's bibliographic and digital objects (available at http://catalog.coloradocollege.edu/) is being built using components of the Catalog Pull Platform's technology stack. The development of the catalog started from a minimum viable product for use by patrons in resource discovery and access; it allows patrons to actively contribute comments and other provenance through annotations, data sets, assessments, and outcomes related to specific linked data bibliographic and authoritative entities. The Colorado College's catalog also gives authenticated users the ability to create, update, replace, or delete information associated with these entities.

Earlier iterations of catalog pull platforms included staff productivity utilities for handling complex or manually intensive workflows. These manual workflows used Colorado College library's legacy ILS and the Islandora and Fedora Commons digital repositories. MARC Batch app is an application that normalizes vendor-provided MARC21 records to conform to cataloging standards and to better interoperate with legacy systems such as an ILS.

This book goes into much technical detail about specific technologies used in implementing catalog pull platforms. The larger points and concepts made in each chapter's case study are explained through the application of specific tools in the development of the Catalog Pull Platform. These examples use the Catalog Pull Platform, which means that they cannot be replicated using other technologies, either open-source or commercial software, by library software developers in libraries and vendors. The design and implementation of the Catalog Pull Platform consciously and deliberately uses lean startup ideas and principles and thus provides concrete examples of a library using lean principles.

1.4 LEARNER AND LIBRARY LEADERSHIP BADGES

To maximize engagement with the book material and to publicize understanding of these lean principles in the library, readers can earn two Open Badges through the book's website. By purchasing this book, all badge fees are waived for an individual to first earn a Learner Badge, followed by the opportunity to earn their Library Leadership badge.

These badges are part of the Mozilla OpenBadge ecosystem, which provides an opportunity for readers to use these badges in documenting their professional development for assessment, evaluation, and tenure processes at their current institution. For newly graduated library school students or those still in school, these badges help signal their knowledge and newly acquired expertise to prospective employers. The Learner and Library Leadership badges can also be added to the reader's LinkedIn and other social networks for professional networking and promotion.

The progression from Learner's Badge to the Library Leadership Badge allows readers to develop and grow by engaging with the material and through contacts and discussion with other readers and participants. All participants in the Library Leadership Badge must first earn their Learner Badge to ensure that all of the participants in the Library Leadership badge cohort have a strong foundation in understanding the concepts, processes, and techniques of lean startup and lean manufacturing in libraries. While the Learner's Badge focuses on explaining these ideas and then testing comprehension of the material in the book, the Library Leadership Badge is much more community- and team-driven. The Learner Badge requirements are completion of a series of quizzes and minimal community participation for each chapter; the Library Leadership Badge expands on that base by requiring the participant to form a small team with other cohorts and complete a project using the ideas and techniques in this book. Other requirements for the Library Leadership Badge include mentoring others in the Learner Badge cohort and participating more extensively in the book's social platform. While the Library Leadership Badge is geared toward midcareer library professionals, it is open to all individuals who successfully earn their Learner Badge.

Supporting your efforts in earning these library badges, an educational and networking badge ecosystem is available at the book's Web site at www.becomingleanlibrary.com/. After registering for an account, readers will be able to comment ongoing topics, watch videos, chat with other learners participating in this program, and take online quizzes toward earning a Learner Badge.

1.5 MEMORY INSTITUTIONS ARE LEARNING ORGANIZATIONS

"Memory institution" is a phrase used frequently to describe libraries, archives, and museums. As Guy Pessach (2000) stated in an article, "Memory institutions are social entities that select, document, contextualize, preserve, index and thus canonize elements of humanity's culture, historical narratives, individual and collective memories. Archives, museums and libraries are paradigmatic examples for traditional memory institutions." While the focus of this book is on libraries, the lean principles and processes can be applied more generally to organizations with a purpose and function combining customer service within the longer-term curation and cultural preservation of artifacts.

A core value of the library profession is the desire to improve access to information in physical, electronic, or any creative hybrid of information artifacts. To continue serving their current and future patrons, libraries face questions about maintaining relevancy in the twenty-first century. Large corporations spend and earn billions of dollars in capturing, indexing, and trying to control the information flow to and from their users. Too often librarians, patrons, and staff have to rely on slow development cycles, poor customer support, and very expensive commercial ILSs. This is slowly changing as these vendors face competition from open-source and non-library-specific alternatives. Library system vendors have an incentive for keeping libraries tied to their legacy systems, even when the more general world of technology innovation is more than several generations ahead of these legacy systems.

In the lean startup and lean manufacturing business literature, startup and established companies are encouraged to transform themselves into learning organizations. A learning organization does more than simply acquiring new skills, technology, or processes; it requires a shift in leadership and organizational culture. A learning organization develops and encourages the ability of its people to learn new skills, capabilities, and knowledge. As exemplified by Toyota (Liker, 2004, p. 251), a learning organization starts from its mistakes and failures by trying to identify and learn the root causes of a problem, taking effective countermeasures to ameliorate the problem, giving individuals the ability and authority to implement the countermeasures, and, finally, ensuring that the knowledge gained through the process is documented and transferred to the correct people in the organization.

Libraries have a deep and enduring tradition of being fundamentally a service industry, driven by the wants, desires, and needs of their patrons. More companies, even those that are in the traditional manufacturing sector, are realizing that they need to shift their perspective from using "push"-focused production (i.e., if you build it, the customers will come) to a "pull" model where the customer or user drives the interactions beyond the first sale of the product.

As Henry Chesbrough states in the foreword to a Deloitte Center for the Edge white paper, "The 2011 Shift Index," "its [the shift from push to pull] implications for thinking about one's business, whether one makes a product or a service, as a service business" (Hagel, Brown, & Kulasooriya, 2011). The authors of this report also observe a business trend that libraries are also struggling with: "Connected individuals, not companies, are the ones harnessing flows and have more power because of it. Declining information asymmetry, lower switching costs, and emerging trends, such as a technology-enabled resources sharing, are increasing Consumer Power and providing additional options for consumption" (Hagel, Brown, & Kulasooriya, 2011, p. 4). Library patrons are constantly being deluged with newer options for their own information needs independent of the library or the online resources provided by the library. Patrons- and admittedly librarians and library staff—use the Internet for most of their reference questions. While people hopefully do use a library's website to access premium online content that is purchased by the library, most of the time they do not think to use the library as their parents or grandparents would have done in years past.

The market for library systems is relatively small: an approximately $1.8 billion a year market for library and related systems (Breeding, 2013). This size market may be one reason there is less incentive for much startup activity within the library automation industry compared with larger technology markets such as social networks, gaming, and mobile devices. Another disincentive for startups in the library technology world is that the market is not expanding, with very few new physical libraries being built, staffed, and funded, although pure digital libraries such as the Digital Public Library of America and HaithiTrust receive funding and other resources.

Open-source development in library technology started maturing in the early to mid-2000s, starting with the Koha ILS in 1999. Individuals working in libraries and as consultants began to work on open-source ILSs with Evergreen in 2005 and later worked on and released open-source discovery layers, starting with VuFind from Villanova University in 2006. The attraction of open-source software to libraries derives partly from the traditional value libraries place on maximizing information availability for their users and patrons. This nascent open-source developer community grew into the first Code4Lib in 2008; with each subsequent year, the conference has grown into a much larger, worldwide community.

Even the most passionate supporters of the current status quo in library technology admit the need for customization of enterprise systems and to integrate them into the existing technology ecosystems in libraries. Starting with what is usually one of its highest costs—a library's ILS or libraries systems platform—other technologies that need to be integrated are the library's digital repository (if it has one), Web site, open URL resolvers, and electronic resource management software. This is in addition to other, more general human resources, accounting, and communication systems that are required for most libraries. This integration is even needed for software that is offered by the same vendor. Integrating all of these disparate items so they work correctly and seamlessly for the library's users requires much manual intervention and monitoring by library staff.

Librarians have a choice about their future as a profession and about the future of libraries. This book is a strong advocate for the position that for libraries to maximize their limited human and financial assets, they need to become lean learning organizations that learn and adopt to changes. While it may be daunting and overwhelming, libraries must create and live a narrative that accommodates and even thrives in this new universe of information overload but the scarce attention of their patrons and users, rather than passively accepting the cultural, technological, economic, and political forces that buffet them library,. Librarians can do better and must if the profession wants to avoid becoming a quaint historical anachronism. Libraries were and are powerful forces for active citizens to participate and enrich democracy and the Enlightenment ideals of educated and informed citizens. The existence to avoid, but that may be becoming an increasingly reality for libraries, is as institutional shells—libraries without any proper and meaningful role in the modern society.

1.6 THE LEAN LEARNING LIBRARY

This book aspires to provide the working librarian or library leader with the tools, philosophy, and approaches to transforming all or part of a library into a lean learning library. While realizing all of the benefits of being lean requires the participation and, more critically, the active engagement of the entire library, these principles can still be adopted and applied by subunits within the library, including the library's technical services and systems departments. This chapters in this book are broken down into the following areas.

Chapter 2, "Organizing Libraries," starts by examining and reviewing the traditional organization of libraries and how to extract the lessons and processes of successful existing libraries. These lessons and processes then are reinterpreted and reapplied within in a lean organizational context. The chapters ends by examining the transformation of the library into a learning organization, powering the success of the individual patron while promoting the success of communities being served by the library.

Chapter 3, "Pull versus Push: Lessons from Lean Manufacturing," starts with an exploration of lean manufacturing, first pioneered by the Japanese automobile company Toyota. Called the Toyota Production System (TPS), it has been widely adopted by many companies and organizations in Asia, the United States, and the rest of the world. This chapter explores a few concepts from TPS. The first TPS concept, called *jidoka*, meaning "automation with a touch," is an approach to understanding and using technology that is based on a hands-on approach that libraries easily appreciate. Another important principle from Toyota is *genchi genbutsu*—understanding from direct experience—an admonishment for library leadership about the value of being directly involved in the core work of the library profession. For helpful advice in managing physical materials inventory, two concepts, *Kanban* and *andon*, applied to libraries offer improvements to existing material workflows and provide options for the coming of smart objects of the Internet of Things. These lessons in techniques and processes, along with a radical shift by the management and leadership of a library, can be applied to libraries and library technology and operations.

Chapter 4, "Build–Measure–Learn as an OODA Loop," introduces the core mechanism used in lean startups to deliver technology products and services in a short amount of time with limited monetary and human resources. This mechanism, called a build–measure–learn loop, is an iterative process that is structurally similar to how the US Military systematically approaches conflict using John Boyd's observe–orient–decide–act (OODA) loop. OODA describes how individual and organizations respond and act while engaging in combat. The build–measure–learn iterative loop is a fundamental tool for the lean library. Concepts from this chapter are the basis for subsequent chapters.

Creating effective and appropriate reporting, tracking, and evaluating statistics is the focus of the Chapters 5, "Innovation Accounting and Francis Taylor." Innovation accounting extends beyond the traditional accrual-based accounting measures of a corporate or nonprofit organization to recognize that measuring the outcomes and process of a library should be integral to the function and evaluation of all service points in the library. Finally, this chapter takes what has been a very traditional approach to the design of many workflow processes in libraries and explains how these workflows can be modified and enhanced through a reinterpretation and restructuring of existing structures to better capture the activity metrics of its patrons and staff.

In Chapter 6, titled "Defining Hypotheses and Managing Complexity," the focus shifts to a neglected but very important step of how to create testable hypotheses for use in a library's build–measure–learn loops. A visualization and hypothesis-generating tool used by lean startups—the *business canvas model*—is applied to libraries, illustrating in a single page the strengths, partners, costs, opportunities, and other elements to help prompt relevant hypothesis. Next, elements of *Olog*, a mathematical notation system, are introduced, and how to use this notation for documenting and communicating the assumptions and expected results of the hypotheses being used in the library is explained. Using this definition makes the complex infrastructure of a library's technology easier to manage and steers change within a library.

In Chapter 7, "Actionable Metrics from Patron Activity," the hypotheses about patron behavior from the previous chapter are now tested through the design, collection, and analysis of the data. This chapter reiterates the importance of using metrics that actually measure or model the behavior of patrons and warns of the lure of vanity metrics that obscure the larger trends occurring in libraries. This chapter lists common sources for patron activity, including ILS reports, COUNTER reports, and the use of Google Analytics. Finally the topic of A/B or cohort testing is introduced; how it has been applied in some examples of technology startups and libraries is described.

Chapter 8, "Pivoting with Technology Change," is about a core concept in lean startups—pivoting—as it is applied to the very different organizational structures that exist in a library. In lean startups, corporations must at times make the hard decision either to continue an existing product or line of business or to shift and pivot to sometimes an entirely different business or product. This decision point for a lean startup is based on the measurements made and hypotheses tested through the build–measure–learn iterative cycles. Libraries cannot easily pivot their primary reason for existing—that of providing information access to their patrons or, in the case of a public library, all different social and economic levels in their communities. Libraries can and should look for specific areas that they can support ,and resources can be reduced so that promising new areas of service, such as digital repositories, the Internet of Things, and makerspaces, as well as being flexible for future roles.

Chapter 9, "DevOps as a Lean Strategy," introduces and explains a recent trend in both large corporations and small businesses of consolidating software development and technology operations into a single unit referred to as DevOps. DevOps offers organizational structures and technological tools that can greatly assist libraries of all sizes to become more lean in their technical services and systems groups. Libraries cannot escape the trend of increased density of electronic services for their patrons, so using DevOps is one strategy to help accomplish this patron and staff demand.

Finally, Chapter 10, "Future as a Warehouse," encourages libraries to reclaim and assert the roles that traditionally have been associated with them while embracing new opportunities for creating, publishing, curating, and managing their communities' creative output. Through lean principles, libraries can pivot toward a better future that centers around the needs and behavior of their patrons. A lean library develops through the serendipitous *creation spaces* for all individuals in the library, while expanding the scopes, types, and communication potentialities when the library's collections shift to *smart collections*.

CHAPTER 2

Organizing Libraries

Many of the problems that plagued our media system before the Internet was widely adopted have carried over into the digital domain—consolidation, centralization, and commercialism—and will continue to shape it.

Taylor (2014)

2.1 TRACKING THE BOOK'S FUTURE

A significant source of the angst experienced by librarians grappling with an uncertain and unknowable future is the radical transformation of reading and the book. As the nature, style, and behavior of readers change with new technology, libraries struggle to respond and adapt to this new reality where printed books are not the focus of most patrons. Dedicated readers, those who spend hours reading literature and genre titles, still purchase, borrow, and consume books at their library.

Some libraries are seeing increasing demand by patrons for eBooks that can be supported on various tablets, smartphones, and dedicated e-reader devices. Companies like Apple, Google, Amazon, and Microsoft funnel their users to purchase commercial content in their various Web storefronts and platforms, and the publishing world is becoming increasingly dependent on the these large commercial avenues as well. Library alternatives are starting to emerge, with the library's focus shifting from managing a print inventory. Libraries are responding to this eBook demand through such programs as the Colorado eBook publishing platform, which are also supporting the creative impulses of their communities through collections that are more dynamic, more local, and paradoxically more global than their print collections.

In his article titled "Post-Artifact Books and Publishing: Digital's Effect on How We Produce, Distribute and Consume Content," Craig Mod outlines how the nature of books has changed. In the traditional book publishing model, reader interaction is at the tail end of a typical book publishing cycle; now readers and communities are active throughout the entire publishing cycle and afterward in social media and other reader venues. The ability and opportunities for reader participation and engagement in all phases of the book publishing cycle now include a long afterlife through reader annotations and conversations about the book.

Becoming a Lean Library
ISBN 978-1-84334-779-8

While Amazon, Goodreads, and Google Books all offer varying levels of support for this rich afterlife of books, libraries need to assert their primary role in this conversation, especially as publishing cycles shorten and reader demands become more capricious and dispersed among so many alternatives.

Bibliographic theory is also changing to better describe the monograph. Starting in the 1990s with the release of the Functional Requirements for Bibliographic Records (usually referred to as FRBR), characteristics of the book were grouped into one of four core classes: work, expression, manifestation, and item. Because these four classes are usually lumped together, a popular shorthand is an anagram of the four together—WEMI. The most general and the most abstract class is the work, an entity that is never physically created but is the most general collection of properties regarding the Book that is independent of a specific physical or digital instance of a book. The next class is the expression, an entity that includes more specific properties such as translation, edition, or other distinctions that differentiate one expression from another expression, although all are expressions of the same work. The third class is manifestation, which includes even more specific properties such as page numbers and identifiers such as the international standard book number. The most specific class is the item, an entity that represents properties of the actual physical item, such as a barcode, price, and other properties that vary between physical items. While FRBR has been extremely influential in bibliographic theory, system development has been much slower; native FRBR library technology is limited to a few experimental systems. FRBR does, however, offer a better framework for partially capturing different properties in the full publishing cycle.

Although library technology vendors have not adopted FRBR, the American Library Association's recent publication of a new cataloging standard, Resource Description and Access (RDA), to replace AACR2, is based on the four levels of the WEMI entities. RDA is a joint publication by the American Library Association, the Canadian Library Association, and the British equivalent, the Chartered Institute of Library and Information Professionals. The goals of RDA cover similar territory as FRBR in that the description of creative endeavors should encourage discovery by patrons through the elimination of abbreviations and by the inclusion of more access points than just author, title, or subject. RDA is slowly being adopted, and library vendors are starting to add RDA-specific tags to the machine-readable catalog (MARC) records.

The intention of replacing AACR2 with RDA has not been without controversy. While critics of RDA and FRBR question the need for a new standard in library bibliographic practice, these changes attempt to track the various characteristics of books as they move through the publishing cycle. What FRBR and RDA lack is a mechanism for tracking and describing the important afterlife of a book after it has been published.

The Library of Congress began a new effort to replace the MARC21 standard for bibliographic and authority entities with a vocabulary and infrastructure that is based on LinkedData principles. They call it BIBFRAME, short for Bibliographic Framework. BIBFRAME also has four fundamental classes but, unlike FRBR, it includes better and more explicit associations between the entities. Instead of four distinct classes to describe various levels of abstraction about a book, BIBFRAME reduces these to two classes: work and instance. The remaining two fundamental classes in BIBFRAME are authority and annotation. The authority class includes statements about the entity creating the work, external subject assignments by catalogers, and organizations involved in the publication and distribution of the instance. The annotation class associates related but distinct statements, such as the instance's cover art, summary, or table of contents, while also providing a mechanism for capturing the postpublication life of the book by allowing people's reviews and comments to be linked with the original work or instance.

In a 2013 report, Roger Schonfeld posed the following questions about the role of eBooks and libraries: "As libraries grapple with a vision for their collections, they face, along with the publishers and distribution partners of these materials, a period of uncertainty. Will digital content platforms develop features and interfaces that provide a compelling alternative to the codex, or will they instead develop a rich role as a complement to the codex?" In either case, if the eBook eventually develops into an alternative that replaces the printed monograph, or if the eBook becomes a complement to a privileged print copy, libraries and library technology needs to support either in libraries' collections of the future.

2.2 POWER AND CULTURE

In the librarian profession, the ideal is that libraries provide a counter to the prevalent dominance of commercial interests: "We do not advance private interests at the expense of library users, colleagues, or our employing institutions" (ALA, 2014). This sixth principle from the American Library

Association code of ethics illustrates a progressive, nonpartisan, and unbiased point of view that libraries would like everyone to embrace as reality.

While these sentiments fulfill a conservative's caricature of a liberal librarian, in the more prosaic analysis of the power structures in a library's culture and administration reflect a realty that is mired in conflicting commercial influences that follows from millions to billions of dollars' worth of advertising. Most librarians would agree in principle with Astray Taylor's (2014, p. 133) contention that libraries support what she calls cultural democracy, which "means that a diversity of voices and viewpoints is expressed and accessible; that influence within the cultural field is achieved by a variety of factors, not simply ceded to those who can afford to pay to be seen and heard."

Within a lean culture, care should be taken that the library's current power structures are not overly represented in favor of commercial, political, or structural elements of what may come next for the library. In the culture of libraries in the past, marginal communities may have had a reduced voice in decisions, such as hiring of library staff, and in adoption of policies and technologies that favored the bias of the dominate culture. Something as simple as the abstract representation of patron services in the signage of the library may reflect the dominate racial and gender majorities of the library's dominate classes and categories, while not being representative of the diversity in the patron communities served by the library.

2.3 THE IMPORTANCE OF DIVERSE VOICES

In subsequent chapters on how to become a lean library that relies on accurate measurements of patrons', staff's, and librarians' interactions and direct feedback, libraries must be mindful always to look toward broadening their communities and the library's organizational structure. This becomes clear when the organizational structure of libraries and library staff are analyzed. Although librarians and staff are in a profession that skews heavily toward women, men are still overly represented in library technology and library systems (Lamont, 2009).

In the context of lean libraries, the challenge is how all library employees, volunteers, and student workers can be empowered to become a knowledge worker. A knowledge worker is a critical problem-solver who contributes to the performance of everyone—not restricted by category but actively seeking expansion of the edges of what constitutes a community member served by the library.

Diversity is also evidenced by not only how libraries encourage the various interests and passions among staff but also how they extend and encourage that interest and passion to library patrons, particularly those library patrons who are already coming to the library with a passion for the subjects they are researching.

2.4 THE LONG TAIL OF LIBRARY SERVICES DEMAND

In a 2005 article, followed by the 2006 book *The Long Tail*, Chris Anderson, the founder of *Wired* magazine, explains how the Internet allows for many more niche marketing opportunities for companies and individuals to tailor their product or service to a small group of users. Through their personal and professional computing devices, people create and maintain multiple presences in formal social networks like Facebook, Twitter, and LinkedIn. The Internet has also drastically changed the availability, access, and discoverabilty of resources at different points along a skewed distribution of people's tastes or preferences. These preferences for the popular follow a power–law distribution, namely that 80% of people's preferences are shared within the same distribution. Libraries—especially public libraries—meet 80% of the demand for bestsellers and what is popular, although there is more competition from other information sources and services to meet this demand for popular materials. Problems with Anderson's conclusions that economic benefits for creators in the long end of the tail is that although the Internet offers access and discoverability of all these items, the economic power and clout are concentrated to just a narrow slice of the winners (Taylor, 2014) (Figure 2.1).

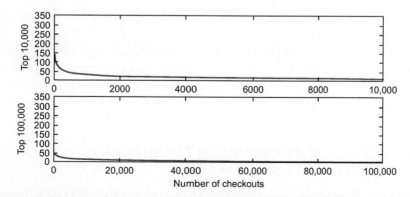

Figure 2.1 Number of checkouts (0–350) of Tutt Library's most popular 10,000 and 100,000 items.

Libraries have always served individuals seeking information on both obscure and well-known topics, particularly when an individual's request for material falls outside the normal distribution of standard requests received most often by reference librarians. As Loren Dempsey (2006) notes in his *D-Lib Magazine* article, "Libraries and the Long Time," this orientation and philosophy to serve all users regardless of the characteristics of their information query goes back to at least Ranganathan's five laws of library science, specifically law 2, which states that "every book has its reader." While this is an aspiration of the library in practice, this means that libraries aspire to meet the information needs of all users, even those with obscure or controversial requests.

Serving individuals on the far edge of the long tail is not always simple. Libraries balance their patrons' demands for popular material while serving those patrons with very specific and distinctly nonmainstream tastes. While there is more competition from other sources and information providers for the popular material, libraries, in defending their resource allocation, rightly point out that they serve everybody regardless of income or technology accessibility that may prevent some patrons from accessing or using alternatives from library competitors. This can put libraries into a catch-22 situation. If the library spends most of their resources and time investing in a broader collection to appeal to larger groups of users, they may deprive access to patrons with much more specific and targeted tastes. The flip side is that if libraries spend more money on the more obscure material, they risk being accused of wasting valuable resources on rarely or never-used content. This tension is certainly not new for libraries. Throughout history, librarians and staff have followed various strategies and processes in their collection development to find a balance between the popular material and material that is more specialized.

Libraries, guided by principles in this book, will be better informed about the demands by patrons for popular material and more responsive to specific requests for material that is farther down the long tail of patrons' information needs and desires.

2.5 MODELS OF INFORMATION TECHNOLOGY DEPARTMENTS IN LIBRARIES

In general, libraries organize their information technology (IT) departments in a fashion similar to that in other equivalent sized commercial and nonprofit organizations. In larger libraries, IT roles and responsibilities are broken down by skill set and function, such as database administrator, network engineer, and application programmer. The promise and hype of cloud computing is that organizations that lack financial and personnel resources, like libraries, can use a cloud service provider to adequately cover all of their responsibilities for technology services without needing to purchase dedicated hardware and to hire employees to support and operate that machinery. Using these distributed, off-site technologies has its risks; libraries often need individuals with specialized skills. In small- and medium-sized libraries, IT is supported by more technological generalists who are responsible for covering multiple areas, often with minimal redundancy in skills between employees.

Another common model for library technology services is a library relying on an external parties for technology services. A public library using the municipal IT department or an academic library using the larger university's IT are both examples of this type of technology service model. While the library does not need as many or expensive IT staff, this arrangement can reduce the library's flexibility in meeting the technology demands of their patrons. The bureaucratic overhead needed to communicate and validate technology services with an external party is an example of this type of reduced flexibility. If the relationship between the library and the external IT group is acrimonious or contentious, the library's technology services becomes even less responsive to patron demands for newer technology or services.

Unfortunately, in such situations, librarians and staff often resort to "back-door" or alternative methods to deliver these technology resources and services. Such duplication of technology increases the costs and overhead of IT for the entire organization. The growth, availability, and ease of use of commercial cloud services such as Amazon, Google, Rackspace, and Microsoft have made this back-door approach even more attractive and easier for libraries seeking to expand their technology services without depending on other units within the larger organization.

A main strength of libraries is their customer service orientation—serving the information needs of the library's patrons; this is increasingly dependent on technology no matter what the size of the library. Being flexible is a trait that should be associated with any library systems group, be it a small library with a single person who is responsible for everything technical, to an established systems department in a large library. Much of the lean startup approach to libraries focuses on the smaller library organization but is easily applied and scaled up for use by larger and more developed systems in larger public and academic libraries.

For libraries, especially larger public and academic libraries, an obvious model for organizational structure follows the pattern of large, late-twentieth-century corporations. As corporations grew larger, they started to experiencing lower costs resulting from economies of scale as employees learned how to better accomplish their jobs; this is sometimes referred to as the experience curve. Economy of scale is the idea that costs for the production of a single product decrease with an increased volume of production. To sustain these larger volumes, corporations needed to become correspondingly larger, with a strict hierarchy and top-down directives to more and different specialized departments within the corporation.

While this model may make sense for manufacturing, large service-based corporations later adopted many of these same structures without necessarily needing all of the specialization required by manufacturing corporations. This organizational model was enormously successful and was a primary driver for economic growth in the twentieth century. As individuals became connected, however, and as information barriers fell away with the Internet and all of its continued disruptions, the model of the top-down, hierarchical corporation that was able to create, forecast, and respond to customers' demands became harder to implement and less effective (Hagel III, Brown, & Davison, 2010, pp. 36–38).

2.6 EVOLUTIONARY AND REVOLUTIONARY CHANGE FOR LIBRARY TECHNOLOGY

While library technology began with the invention of libraries, library technology as a topic distinct from the library itself really did not become obvious until the middle of the nineteenth century with the standardization of cataloging practice, beginning with Sir Anthony Panizzi. Panizzi's *91 Cataloging Rules* provided guidance for generations of librarians and helped standardize the descriptions of books and other printed material.

While library card catalogs were initially created in late in eighteenth-century France by using the back of playing cards, an recognizable precursor was Harvard University Library's early card catalog. Later, Melvin Dewey's contributions to library systems and library technology extend beyond his famous cataloging standard to his efforts in standardizing the fairly typical author, subject, title card catalogs into 3-inch × 5-inch cards with dedicated shelving. In an early example of vendor lock-in, Dewey's company was for libraries the main supplier of these 3 × 5 cards that supported the Dewey card catalog technology. The development and adoption of the Library of

Congress subject headings were an early alternative to the Dewey Decimal System. By the beginning of the twentieth century, most libraries had card catalogs with technical services and circulations operations geared to very manual processes for maintaining a physical card catalog that accurately reflected the collections while offering patrons access to the primarily print material in the library.

In his 1995 report "Online Catalog Design Models: Are We Moving in the Right Direction?," Charles Hildreth reported on the state of electronic catalogs in the 1990s. He identifies two design models used in the integrated library systems (ILS) or online public access catalog (OPAC). The first user interface design was based on a graphical user interface that attempted to emulate the card catalog, a technology known by patrons, librarians, and staff. The second interface emulated the search conventions of commercial databases like DIALOG. Some online catalogs attempted to combine the two design models into a single interface (Hildreth, 1995). Even more than 20 years after Hildreth's report was written, the library catalog still retains one or both of these design models, especially for operations done by the library staff. Modern catalogs and discovery services by major vendors attempt to copy commercial search services, particularly Google and, to a lesser extent, Microsoft's Bing, as well as Amazon's online shopping site.

Libraries can position themselves as the publisher and principal curator of the unique content produced by the communities they serve. This expands the scope of library technology to include the actual digital object instead of a proxy record. This gives rise to digital material, acquired either through purchasing or through donation, or created and produced by the community being served by the library. As Rick Anderson (2013) noted in an editorial, the importance of special collections increases in the environment where most information sources become commodities that can be acquired for minimal costs. Expanding to include research artifacts, such as small data sources and databases—or, as Dorothea Salo (2010) calls them, "small data"—offers another opportunity for libraries to collect, curate, and publish through their digital infrastructure. Most libraries do not necessarily need to worry about the largest data sets (commonly referred to as "big data" in the popular media and blogosphere) but can focus on the myriad of small data sets that are being produced by local sensors, historians, scholars, and other creators in the library's community. By offering to their patrons low-cost or free services for managing and extending these small data sets and new creative products, the library continues in its curation role while becoming more important to their communities. Libraries can provide unique services that cannot matched nor are offered by commercial or non-profit organizations.

Libraries, like many organizations disrupted by the Internet, with its networked and cheap computing devices, have lost their previous stature as the primary information source for their communities. To avoid becoming dinosaurs and a nostalgic footnote in history, library have to evolve and change. This is not because libraries have not embraced technology; many of the library's services area *require* technology. Providing free Internet access to its patrons, purchasing large digital collections, and sharing resources with other institutions are all directly technological or depend on technology to function smoothly. Libraries increase their considerable goodwill and reputation by offering an alternative for preserving and maintaining access to a wider range of physical and digital material. This could include such activities as cataloging works and instances of rapidly produced three-dimensional printing of items in communal makerspaces, or capturing the academic scholarly artifacts as part of open access mandates by government or private grant agencies.

All types of libraries should embrace this new world of abundance, including physical three-dimensional items, online textual material, raw data sets, and become a library for this new century. The hyperlocal should automatically be associated with being able to visit a library, either in person or virtually. The wide range of a library's local collections is now accessible and available to a worldwide audience through the library's digital services. This ability to share, use, and reimagine the library's material is one of the institution's greatest services. Libraries should not be scared of these new opportunities but should embrace them—as revolutionary as some of these ideas are—and become much leaner in operation but much grander and expanded in terms of the type and diversity of their collections.

2.7 CATALOG PULL PLATFORM CASE STUDY FOR ORGANIZING LIBRARY SYSTEMS

The Catalog Pull Platform had its origin in the technical services and systems departments at Colorado College's Tutt Library. The Tutt Library is a rather small academic library, with 10 librarians and approximately 30 staff who primarily serve the needs of a small liberal arts college's faculty, staff, and students. The Tutt Library's various collections include monographs, serials (both electronic and print), video (streaming, DVDs, and a legacy collection of VHS tapes), audio (CDs and LPs), various smaller collections in the library's special collections, government documents, and a separate music library. The total number of the collection is over one million distinct items.

The Tutt Library's organizational structure is flat; all librarians report directly to the director. All of the librarians are expected to staff the reference help desk on a weekly basis, with at least one 4-h shift; most librarians have two or more reference shifts a week. Staffing the reference desk also uses a small number of on-call reference librarians who typically work a couple of shifts during the week and on Saturdays.

The Tutt Library's circulation department has four full-time staff members and a varying number of student workers who assist the staff. Cataloging is done by two full-time staff members along with other staff members with cataloging responsibilities in serials, government documents, special collections, and the music library. Electronic resources and serials has one full-time librarian assisted by one full-time staff member. The library systems department is similarly staffed, with one full-time librarian and one full-time staff member. The rest of technical services is overseen by one librarian with a number of full- and part-time staff members either reporting directly to the librarian or reporting to a middle layer of staff supervisors. Library instruction is spread out among all of the librarians, with one librarian coordinating the library's instruction efforts with the college's faculty and students.

As in many libraries, the Tutt Library's technology stack is a mixture of commercial and open-source software. This software runs on the library's virtual machines on campus and through a number of vendor-hosted applications. The Tutt Library's commercial ILS is hosted in the vendor's data center. The ILS previously ran on a dedicated server in the library's basement and required separate maintenance contracts along with dedicated staff support. Other services, such as gathering reference and instruction statistics, is another application hosted by a separate vendor. The library's Web site is part of the larger campus content management systems; the library's discovery layer and other experimental services are hosted on Linux virtual machines through the campus IT division's larger virtual machine infrastructure. The Tutt Library's digital repository is hosted and managed through a regional consortium. Finally, the library systems group is responsible for maintaining all of the library's computer labs, both Windows PC and Macintosh computers, along with the computers of librarians and library staff.

The precursor to the Catalog Pull Platform started in 2010 with the development of an online application that allows Colorado College seniors to submit their thesis or capstone project directly to the library's hosted Fedora Commons server. The initial development used Linux virtual machines through Django and a number of open-source software libraries from Emory University. The first iteration of the thesis was developed for the economics and business department at Colorado College and was a success, with over 50 theses submitted. In the second and third years the number of college departments expanded to include most of the campus; further user interface and usability enhancements were done in an iterative fashion each year. In the second and subsequent years, the thesis submission application was folded into the library's open-source discovery layer (built by the author). The discovery layer started as a branch of an abandoned open-source project based on Django and was further developed to be roughly equivalent in functionality to other open-source discovery systems such as Blacklight and VuFind.

Two events, occurring within a few months of each other, caused a minor pivot in the development of open-source library systems at Tutt Library. The first was when the main developer and author of this book, Jeremy Nelson, started researching and experimenting with an open-source key-value data store called Redis. The second was when the librarians at Tutt Library expressed an interest in an online bookshelf, similar in design and functionality as a virtual book-browsing widget developed by Stanford University in their open-source implementation of Blacklight. Their solution involved a lot of customization of Solr and Blacklight, which would have been difficult to implement in Tutt Library's new discovery layer.

Unlike Solr, Redis offered a number of advantages, including easier development of the necessary data structures to support the book browser as well as a more flexible manner for storing such data structure primitives as associative arrays, sets, lists, and sorted sets. By combining just the data structures that were needed to support the book browser, other searching possibilities such as strict Boolean queries were now possible. While Solr is excellent at providing a modern search index, the type of Boolean queries that the librarians and staff wanted was not as easy to provide with Solr's complex configuration.

During the next year and a half, the library continued experimenting with Redis. This work was highlighted in a presentation at ALA 2013 Annual Conference as one of the first library systems to natively support the new BIBFRAME vocabulary being actively developed by the Library of Congress. During this time period, some limitations of Redis started to become apparent; the biggest issue was that the entire Redis data store resides in the random access memory (RAM) of the server. Redis transfers its data to disk either at a regular, set interval or every time the data changed in the RAM. Either way, the virtual machines that were available for the project did not have enough RAM to store Colorado College's entire collection of MARC records in Redis. While using Redis did offer very fast response times to queries, the library experimented with various ways to try to get the entire collection of MARC records, including sharing Redis instances among other virtual machines and trying to leverage a computer lab running multiple Redis instances in the background.

Because of the small size of the systems department at Tutt Library, the development of the Redis-based bibliographic system languished because of the library's other priorities. The library started a concerted effort to increase the use of its Fedora Commons–based digital repository through aggressive solicitation of digital artifacts being produced by the college's different offices, departments, and communities. Effort shifted to developing lightweight tools to improve the productivity of library staff working on ingesting material into the digital repository. To minimize the different technology stacks that the systems department needed to support, all of the Redis and Fedora programs developed were standardized using a Django-based project called Aristotle Library Apps.

A concentrated effort was made to decouple the different modules from dependence on each other in the Aristotle Library Apps project. Changes made to the Fedora Commons utilities did not affect the Redis functionality of the existing apps. However, the hard limits of available RAM in the college's virtual machines encouraged research into other NoSQL technologies; the college finally decided to use Fedora 4 to store the LinkedData RDF, Redis for results caching and analytics, and Elastic Search for search and access.

CHAPTER 3

Pull versus Push: Lessons from Lean Manufacturing

3.1 QUICK PRIMER ON LEAN MANUFACTURING

The beginnings of the lean manufacturing started before World War II with the founding of Toyota Motor Works by Kiichiro Toyoda as an extension of his father's company, Toyota Industries. Toyota first copied the techniques of the assembly line manufacturing process that was introduced and popularized in the early twentieth century by Henry Ford and the Ford Motor Company. By building large factories for the direct assembly of cars, along with the manufacturing of parts by subcontractors, Ford realized large economies of scale whereby the average cost per car was reduced through shear size of its massive operations.

Toyota, by contrast, did not have the capital or infrastructure to copy Ford's success by building large factories. Toyota had to look at alternative methods to manufacture cars in the absence of the assembly line infrastructure of Ford, General Motors, or other large automotive manufactures in the United States that, along with the supporting automotive part plants, together formed the core of the automotive industries in the early twentieth-century United States.

Before Toyota's development of a set of principles and practices that became the basis for the lean manufacturing movement, most car manufacturing used variations of Henry Ford's assembly line. Each station on an assembly line was responsible for adding a single part or a set of related automobile parts to the incomplete car as it progressed through the line. The goal of manufacturing a car in an assembly line is to increase the volume of manufactured cars while trying to maintain consistency in car quality. Each station on the manufacturing line "pushes" the results of their piece to the next station, regardless of the product or outcome in a previous station of the assembly line.

The worst situation for any individual station is to hold up the assembly line, thereby preventing the completion of the final finished automobile. In such an assembly line manufacturing setup, each station on the line can become a source of failure; any work stoppage forces a shutdown of the entire process of product production. Managers in the traditional assembly

Becoming a Lean Library
ISBN 978-1-84334-779-8

line try to ensure that the stations under their control are not the source of any work stoppage, creating an incentive for the manager to keep the assembly line moving forward even if quality issues or problems emerge in the manufacturing of the automobile. In the traditional assembly line, quality control is usually done by inspecting the finished product. When critical problems in the quality of the finished goods are identified, expensive retrofitting of the assembly line may be required or, if the problems are minor, the problems may be ignored.

Push-based systems, including Ford's and most types of manufacturing companies, grew and prospered because of a few reinforcing trends based on product marketing assumptions and the size of the enterprises. These trends and assumptions proved to be successful for most of the twentieth century and continued into the twenty-first. The first assumption of push-based systems is that customer demand can be accurately predicted so that strategic planning of the firm's operations can be designed and resources allocated to meet that demand. In this environment where demand is stable and predicable, the corporation that grew larger could realize economies of scale by becoming bigger as variable costs per unit of product drop with corresponding larger profits that are realized by the firm when more products are sold. As corporations grew in size, extensive hierarchies developed within the corporation to control its complex operations, with all of the strategic decisions being made by an elite few who stood at the apex or top of the hierarchy. Variability in a corporation's manufacturing operations was a problem that required extensive controls to minimize; this then moved that philosophy into other aspects of the corporation. Another assumption of push-based systems is that the corporation was involved in a zero-sum game with other corporations because the customer demand was limited and, by necessity, the customer could choose only one product at a time.

The central assumption of push-based systems—that demand can be accurately forecast—meant that businesses could predict demand and respond accordingly. This allowed for stable growth of a corporation while also leading to the expansion of the marketing and advertising departments. These departments' purpose was to create, control, and manipulate the demand for the corporation's products and services. This, coupled with natural geographic and informational barriers, limited consumers' choices in accessing and ordering products and services. These limitations of customer information and access made it easier for the corporation to predict and meet the customers' demand while also encouraging the expansion of the corporation's size and complexity.

The dominant push model started breaking down because of two forces that started gathering steam at the end of the twentieth century. The first was the rapid improvement in computing power that, in a relatively short time, gave the average individual access to increasingly powerful portable machines. The second force was the implementation and spread of packet-based networking technology that started connecting these computers to each other regardless of a person's geographical location (Hagel III, Brown, & Davison, 2010, p. 43). With computing power increasing in such dramatic fashion, coupled with packet-based networking, an individual's demand has fragmented across a much larger range of choices that are not necessarily restricted by barriers such as geography or ignorance about alternatives. With so many options and choices, an individual's preferences and demand for goods are no longer as easily predictable as they had been in the past.

One of the promises being made in the recent hype about "Big Data" is that these vast archives of individuals' online behavior being captured will restore corporations' ability to better predict and respond to customer demand for the corporation's products and services.

Push-oriented marketing and advertising departments in large corporations become less effective and more expensive with less certainty, making the extensive planning and operations of twentieth-century corporations much more difficult to implement over the reduced time frames that were accelerated by global competition and consolidation of Web-based marketing avenues to a few large corporate behemoths.

In contrast to a push-based system, in a pull-based system each individual station of the assembly line waits until an upstream station requires its intermediary products before beginning work. The individual station produces only what is demanded from the upstream processes; essentially, work begins only when its outputs are "pulled" by upstream demand. This allows the factory or manufacturing plant to support more variation in the product line, even up to the point where each product is completely customized to meet the specific demands of the customer. Quality control in the pull system includes both automated and manual inspections that check for problems as the incomplete product flows through an individual station. If deficits or problems are discovered, the station shuts down and manufacturing does not continue until the problem is addressed by either the front-line employees working at that stations or, if the problem is more serious, a response team comprising managers and engineers. A further consequence of this pull-based system is that amount of work in progress and finished goods inventories are minimized.

While this works well for some types of services and manufacturing companies, Toyota and other large manufactures allow small buffers of incomplete product to accumulate so that if a shutdown on the line does occur, the buffers allow the manufacturing process to continue for short time while the problem is addressed. This small-batch approach may fail if the shutdown to fix problems takes a significant amount of time; upstream stations can quickly run out of their small buffer stock.

3.2 THE PAST AS A SERIES OF PUSH PROCESSES

The push model of production method is not very flexible or responsive to rapid changes in customer demand. In a traditional manufacturing operation, it is difficult for the same factory or assembly line to manufacture multiple product lines, even if product lines are similar. This is because in a traditional manufacturing process, any deviation of the product requires the employees to retool or modify the existing machinery or tools to accommodate the different product. A consequence of this rigidity in the manufacturing process is that the company restricts customer choice to a few models. The expense of constantly changing the manufacturing environment is too high to justify the marginal increase in sales from a company offering a wide range of products or to allow for individual customization of the product.

Push is more than just a manufacturing technique; push perspectives and practices permeate the world. Push as the dominate model in most areas of people's lives started with the Industrial Revolution in the eighteenth century. The authors of *The Power of Pull* explain the assumptions and practices behind push: "Push operates on a key assumption—that is possible to forecast or anticipate demand" (Hagel et al., 2010, p. 34). For library leaders, much effort and time are spent trying to anticipate the demands for services and resources by the library's patrons. While this may have been a successful strategy in an environment where access to information resources was limited by cost and physical location, in the new world of instant information access through digital devices, trying to anticipate and predict patron demand becomes harder and more expensive. Push programs improperly assume that basic humans can be scripted and predicted, and that people are not generally creative or talented or have complex motivations and desires.

Table 3.1 compares and contrasts push programs with pull platforms.

Trying to script or map out a workflow that completely anticipates the demand for a product or service involves extensive "command-and-control"

Table 3.1 Push Programs verses Pull Platforms

Push Programs	Pull Platforms
Demand can be anticipated	Demand is highly uncertain
Top-down design	Emergent design
Centralized control	Decentralized initiative
Procedural	Modular
Tightly coupled	Loosely coupled
Resource centric	People centric
Participation restricted to few participants	Participation open to many diverse participants
Efficiency focus	Innovation focus
Limited number of major reengineering efforts	Rapid incremental innovation
Zero-sum rewards	Positive-sum rewards
Extrinsic rewards dominate	Intrinsic rewards dominate

Source: From Push to Pull: Emerging Models for Mobilizing Resources (Hagel et al., 2010, p. 99).

operations with comprehensive step-by-step plans that must followed by individuals in the organization. Deviations from these scripted workflows requires the organization to handle or manage the inevitable outliers or exceptional circumstances. This becomes increasingly difficult as these plans grow in size and complexity. In traditional top-down corporate hierarchies, decisions for allocating resources and people are made to meet these forecasted demands. The process of allocation within the organization becomes highly political as different areas try to appropriate resources for their respective divisions within the organization. In libraries, this top-down approach to meeting patron demand creates an environment where the library's senior staff may jockey for position and increased funding because of their assumption of passive and steady demand for library resources by patrons.

For academic libraries, public libraries, and K-12 school libraries, the larger institution's bureaucracy, workflow, and even basic assumptions all first were conceived and developed using the logic and practices of the dominant, push-based corporations that flourished in the twentieth century. These assumptions and practices can hamper a library as it attempts to shift from push-based to pull-based operations and collections. With budgets, personnel, and services being decided by larger institutions' upper management and leaders, libraries traditionally may have had limited opportunities to structure their operations and services in radical fashion.

The challenge for the leadership of a lean library is to gain the freedom to explore pull-based operations and services while still being responsive and accountable to the larger institution. The larger institution may still be a push–based organization, but the library may be able to adopt and operate using lean principles centered around pull processes. Trying to bridge the traditional push-based expectations and practices—where all important decisions are made by a small cadre of senior management and imposed in a top–down fashion—with an alternative pull-based organization is continued challenge. Giving front-line employees the support and freedom to change and adapt to the needs and desires of patrons is not an easy nor a necessarily fast process.

There are reasons for optimism, and libraries are not alone in these challenging times. Most institutions, no matter what type, are also struggling in this new world of varied and multiple demands by customers. By providing leadership and being supportive and communicative about the success of pull-based workflows in the library, library leadership can create openings within the larger institutions for new models of operations. By recognizing that the challenges of trying to respond to patrons' more varied and changing demands is also shared by other types of organizations, libraries can identify, adopt, and then customize the best practices and processes that are developing in reaction to patrons' variable demand for information resources and services.

3.3 THE GROWTH AND DEVELOPMENT OF PULL

In a "pull" model, manufacturing is dependent on the demand of upstream production, eventually finishing with the end customer's purchase. For example, take a simplified manufacturing process whereby a company produces an imaginary widget requiring three steps in an assembly line before the widget is ready for retail purchase by the customer. The first step takes the raw materials and converts them into a widget shell, the second step assembles the internal parts of the widget, and the third step involves applying a coat of paint and adding the final external parts to the widget. In a traditional push manufacturing process, the first step continually builds the widget shell and passes the shell to the second step, even if the second step is behind in assembling the internal parts. Figure 3.1 illustrates the differences between push and pull models in manufacturing.

3.3.1 Push and Pull Manufacturing Processes

In a pure pull process, none of the three steps are started until the customer orders a widget. From this order, the third step sends its requirements to the

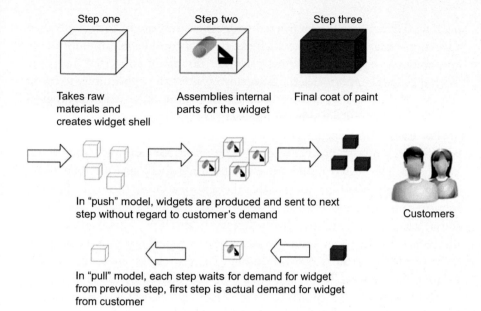

Figure 3.1 Push versus pull manufacturing models.

second step, and only when the second step is ready to assemble the internal parts does the first step begin manufacturing the widget shell. A manufacturer practicing a lean process does not keep the factory running in the absence of orders for the product; production starts only when orders arrive. If a manufacturer supplies an intermediary part for a larger product, the lean manufacturing process remains the same, with production starting only when it receives order from an upstream supplier.

A second important focus of lean manufacturing is minimizing waste in the flow of the entire production process. Sources of waste include excess materials inventory, partially constructed parts, or in the final packing that is discarded after the customer's purchase of the product. Going back to the previous widget example, a push process tends to overproduce widget shells in the first step as workers continually build the widget shells out of the raw materials inventory until the materials are exhausted. If the second step in the widget manufacturing cannot handle all these constructed widget shells from the first step, these widget shells must be stored and tracked until the second step is ready. If the second step produces too many raw widgets for the third step to handle, these incomplete widgets also require storage, handling, and tracking. These partially constructed widgets accumulate in each step, called a work-in-progress inventory, which can tie up a considerable amount of the corporation's money and resources that are not easily converted into cash. With these large inventories, the company "wastes" the opportunity to invest or grow as their money and materials are tied up in these work-in-progress inventories in the manufacturing process.

For service organizations such as libraries, the push model begins with a patron searching for resources from home using, for example, Google and Wikipedia. The search results from the patron's query include links to an article from a professional journal that the patron accesses through a library's subscription database. The final step is the patron accessing the article through a database purchased by the library. In this typical discovery process, the patron might never directly interact with the library's home page or discovery layer but does depend on being able to access the online article through the technology services purchased and offered by the library.

The Toyota Motor Company—as the originator of lean manufacturing—created a philosophy and process for lean manufacturing called the Toyota Production System (TPS). The TPS is based on five core concepts (Womack & Jones 2003):
- Defining customer value
- Defining the value stream
- Making it "flow"
- "Pulling" from the customer back through the production process
- Striving for excellence

By reformulating these concepts as questions specific to libraries, the TPS core concepts can still be useful if reformulated with a service perspective:
- When defining customer value, what value is the library to the patron?
- What processes or workflows in the library provide that value to the library?
- How can the library make the value stream more seamless with less friction from library operations?
- Where are the library's patrons using these services, and how can patron desires and needs be captured with the library responding to those demands in its workflows?
- What are the metrics and outcomes that demonstrate that the library is meeting or exceeding patrons' demands for resources and services?

All five of the TPS core concepts reflect a shift in how a library responds to customers' or patrons' desire for services or resources. Although a library is not a direct manufacturer of materials (although a case could be made that, with the introduction of print-on-demand services and makerspaces, libraries directly publish or "manufacture" books or three-dimensional objects based on a patron's desire), by being an intermediary and curator, a library functions more efficiently if the focus is on the patron through the processes and operations of providing library services and resources to the patron.

While many companies over the past couple of decades have adopted lean principles, some of these companies fail to realize all of the benefits of TPS because their implementation of lean manufacturing is superficial and does not fully implement all five core concepts of the TPS. Without an organization's senior leadership fully supporting all of the changes necessary to shift the culture of the company when adopting lean principles, the benefits of such an approach may not be apparent or obvious. Front-line employees who are less engaged and who believe that library management is not committed to lean philosophy likely will not actively seek ways for improving patron flow through creative and active engagement with the production streams or service workflows. Changing the culture and traditional management in libraries requires the commitment to implement lean principles by the library's leadership.

Pull operations have existed within larger push-based companies and organizations for a long time. For example, an emergency department in a hospital functions as a pull operation. Health emergency services are purely driven by demand, with health remediation not even starting until an individuals enters the hospital doors. Doctors, nurses, and other health professionals responding to the health emergency can mobilize an incredible amount of resources, including specialists and technology, to stabilize and treat their patient. Although never as dramatic as an emergency department, demand for library services may function as a pure pull platform. Similar to how an emergency department must be ready to treat immediately a wide range of health emergencies, most patron demands for a library's references, interlibrary loan (ILL), and collections, both physical and electronic, often start with the individual either entering the library or accessing online the library-mediated electronic resources. For most situations, reference and electronic services should be available to library patrons as they demand it, regardless of whether the patron is physically in the library or is using the library's online services.

In libraries, much like in established manufacturing companies, half-heartedly applying lean manufacturing principles makes it difficult to realize the benefits of the lean philosophy in the organization. While the goals and purposes of a library are different from for-profit manufacturing companies, both types of organizations can benefit from the philosophy and approach of TPS. The opportunity for libraries to more efficiently use their limited resources to meet their mission is possible. Quality and excellence in library services, flowing from the library's service function, are more difficult to define, measure, and react to than a physical product resulting from a lean manufacturing factory. Too much of library decision making is done with the absence of meaningful metrics and often demonstrates a surprising lack of knowledge about the specifics of the day-to-day workflows and processes in the working library.

3.4 APPLYING JIDOKA AND HEIJUNKA: EXAMPLES OF LEAN PRINCIPLES

Sakichi Toyoda, the founder of the industrial group that would later become the Toyota Industries, pioneered an idea called jidoka, roughly translated as "automation with a human touch." Jidoka, as applied by Toyota and other lean manufacturers, tries to design machinery that builds quality into the product, such that if the product does not pass inspection, the machine stops working until intervention by a human. This is also referred to as autonomation, or equipment endowed with human intelligence to stop itself when it has a problem (Liker, 2004, p. 129).

A jidoka approach to library services does not attempt to replace a library's staff but to provide better tools for fulfilling the information demands of its patrons. For example, a library with an online reference chat service may want to configure their chat software such that it requires an active connection to a librarian or staff, and if they are not available, the chat service does not work.

Using a lean approach for library services, it is the patron who initiates the demand for a resource or service. In Chapter 7, this notion of the patron, or end user, as the driver for the service or resource is expanded in more detail. A library following push-based processes and services—where a librarian forecasts and makes assumptions about patrons' information needs—attempts to organize its operations around those predictions. By contrast, pull-based operations elevate and promote the individual patron, even when the patron is unclear about their information need.

To effectively serve their communities, libraries must be able to provide a consistently high level of customer service, even if the demand for customer service varies considerably over a typical day or week. While many library services can be seen as "build to order," that is, completely dependent on the patron's desires, like traditional reference and resource-sharing, the library may want to consider implementing **heijunka**, another idea from lean manufacturing where volume and product mix in a production line are leveled out by workers manufacturing products at a consistent and predictable rate.

Although heijunka is more applicable within a manufacturing enterprise, service organizations like libraries can modify their operations in two ways: fit patron demand into a leveled service schedule and establish consistent times for different types of services (Liker, p. 123). Libraries already do both in many instances; for example, most libraries schedule consistent dates and times for staff reference or other service points as a way to level the services provided. While time estimates for certain services are usually ad hoc and inconsistent, libraries that over time have captured metrics regarding their services can start doing a better job estimating the duration of any individual service and then begin scheduling staff time according to that analysis.

3.5 GENCHI GENBUTSU

In the TPS, two concepts—**genchi genbutsu** and **kaizen**—are important lean principles with relevant applications in libraries. The first, genchi genbutsu, is the idea that an individual cannot understand the circumstances and context of a situation without observing the process firsthand. Genchi, roughly translated as "actual location," and genbutsu, translated as the actual materials or products, is a central tenet in the TPS. Genchi genbutsu requires more than a cursory examination of a process; it requires deep focus by concentrating on the "why" behind the workflow or process. First examining the reasoning behind a process, then observing to see whether the actual practice aligns with the outcomes based on the previous reasoning, is central to genchi genbutsu. A significant consequence of Toyota placing such an emphasis on personal understanding and experience of process is that the individual who is now responsible for the information and analysis directly reports to supervisors and other interested parties. Another corollary that Toyota makes explicit with genchi genbutsu is encouraging organizational knowledge flows using the experience and wisdom of others in a process because of their direct, personal involvement with the work being done.

How can senior leadership in a library practice genchi genbutsu given the multiple and varied demands on their time and energy? Another practice from Toyota and other Japanese businesses can help: **hourensou** is actually an amalgamation of three Japanese terms. Hourensou is the practice of requiring frequent reports from subordinates that summarize the latest results from their responsibilities and also includes warnings about potential problems related to their roles in the organization. If the subordinates are using genchi genbutsu for the situations and workflows that they are responsible for, their reports should reflect a deeper understanding and observation of the processes behind the work.

Taking the concept of hourensou to social networks and mobile devices, communication between a direct report and supervisor can be done through instant messenger, video chats, and even e-mail. When using social networks, care should be taken not to inadvertently release publicly sensitive or potentially damaging information to the supervisor. As these alternatives guide the organization through the frequent changes and demands of their customers, not just the data and analytics are discussed, but also the facts observed by the empowered individual should encourage information flow back and forth between the library's leadership. Genchi genbutsu is about understanding and developing trust in the library's staff through increasing engagement by taking a more reflective and direct view of process and workflow.

Leaders in libraries should not allow themselves to be too far removed from the core mission of the library, that is, serving the information needs of their patrons. Leaders who experience front-line interactions with library patrons is putting genchi genbutsu into practice. This does not mean that library leaders need to spend an inordinate amount of time directly experiencing and observing how their library is accomplishing a task. Instead, the intent of the leader is getting out and observing while actively engaging in all aspects of the various service areas in the library. This sends strong signals to the front-line library staff about the importance of their work and, as a learning organization, empowers their own decision making that is based on data and direct facts from their workflows.

3.6 KAIZEN

The second lean principle from the TPS is *kaizen*, incompletely translated as "continuous improvement," whereby the organization develops processes and procedures that encourage the development of institutional knowledge through individuals learning from mistakes made in manufacturing or service delivery. In his book on Toyota's lean principles, Liker mentions that for Toyota, standardization and innovation are complementary. Individual or group innovation at Toyota comes from the ability to transfer the knowledge and process from innovation to the wider company because of Toyota's ability to standardized and communicate throughout the organization (Liker, p. 251). For many first reading this statement about innovation, it may be difficult to reconcile, particularly with the common mass media narrative that innovation is about an individual achieving results in conflict with organizational barriers and inertia. What Toyota provides is the rationale and means for an individual's or small group's creative spark or idea to spread through and improve the larger organization. Toyota's kaizen practice is about integrating incremental or small improvements; while they may not rise to the level of a significant game-changer, when viewed across the entire company, they show an environment that encourages innovation. Toyota builds organizational structures and practices to easily integrate new knowledge about improvements into standards in the company. These minor improvements in processes and practices then allow Toyota to propagate them throughout the company in a consistent and orderly fashion.

Unlike other companies that penalize employees when mistakes or breakdowns occur, Toyota views any problem as an opportunity to improve and learn from the situation. This starts with trying to understand the root cause of the problem, which requires further reflection to go beyond the apparent cause and effect of a problem and more deeply investigate why the problem occurred, or its root cause. Toyota's process is not a sophisticated statistical or technological marvel, but it ultimately comes down to what is called the "five whys"—basically taking a problem and asking why that problem occurred, then, after getting an explanation, again asking why about the underlying causes. Through this iterative process, each previous answer is examined for causes until the root cause is determined. In Toyota's five-why process, this process of asking why about the explanation occurs at least five times when individuals are trying to tease out the underlying causes of a problem. A library example can help to illustrate Toyota's five whys in action and explain this technique. A common problem in academic libraries is when a patron experiences difficulty accessing an article from one of the library's purchased article databases. Each iteration elicits additional questions about the reason for the previous answer.

- The answer to the first "Why?" is because the patron was using the wrong URL when trying to access a journal article.
- The answer to the second "Why?" is asked to determine why the patron was using the wrong URL. The reason is because she did a Web search for the resource.

- The answer to the third "Why?" is because the patron did not know that the URL from the Web search was not correctly proxied for the library's database. The correct URL is accessible from the library's Web site.
- The answer to the fourth "Why?" is that the process for accessing remote resources from the library's Web site is not clear, and that the proxied URL is not made obvious.
- The answer to the final "Why?" of the problem of a patron not being able to access the resource is because the library's Web site design has not been updated recently and that the current design obfuscates the process for accessing the library's purchased online resources.

For libraries interested in adopting kaizen in their own operations, the five-why approach is a very detailed and painstaking process for analysis. It requires concentration and time, along with a willingness of the library leadership to figure out the root causes of the problem that started a chain reaction of issues leading up to the reporting of the problem. Toyota's problem-solving kaizen process results in continuous improvement by first identifying and clarifying the initial problem to determine the actual location or point of concern of the problem, followed by an iterative five-why analysis to finally identify the root cause of the problem. Once this root cause is found, countermeasures are implemented and then evaluated to ensure they adequately address the root cause. Only after the root cause has been effectively addressed does Toyota then take those successful countermeasures and standardize the problem-solving approach for use across the company. This standardization of problem solutions is a critical part of Toyota's problem-solving process and reinforces and supports a culture of organization learning.

In Japanese culture, and at Toyota in particular, a practice and a mind-set called **hansei** enables the most effective use of kaizen. Roughly translated as "reflection," hansei is the attitude that an individual is accountable for any problems and that the individual should reflect and discuss this weakness so that the problem can be addressed and rectified. While hansei has been interpreted as just negative feedback, the more accurate view is that hansei is a mechanism for an individual to improve from a negative situation, and as a tool for organizational improvement as well. Hansei is about reflection on the process and about the errors or problems that occurred (Kopp, 2010). Unlike modern attitudes that focus on constant positive reinforcement, which can even go as far as ignoring weaknesses and focusing too much on an individual's strengths, hansei is the opposite attitude. While hansei in libraries likely would not be acceptable to many staff or librarians, the hansei principle is useful for library leadership to redirect focus on the process when there occurs a failure in how library services are delivered or in the collections.

3.7 IMPROVING THE FLOW OF PATRON SERVICES

By looking at their services from a flow perspective, libraries can discover improvements for even well-used and efficient processes. By focusing on how many points at which a patron interacts with the library, both virtually and in person, the removal of duplicate points in the library's functions, along with improvement in the efficiency of each service point combine to reduce the time required by and to improve the flow of the patron using the service. For example, a typical process of a patron finding a book would involve the following service points:

- First, the patron discovers the book in the library's catalog,
- Second, the patron locates the book on the library's shelf,
- Third, the patron stands in line to check out the book.

The flow of the patron and the number of times the patron interacts with the library is at least three but likely more. Unlike a restaurant or retail establishment, the library does not need to balance the customer's time in the store with the optimal flow of customers' traffic through the business.

What a library does share with a restaurant or retail store is improving its service to customers by reducing the friction and frustration a patron may experience while moving between the library's various service points. If the patron is unable to locate a book or if the physical layout of the library is confusing, this has a cost in effectiveness for patrons using the library. A library process like the one described above should be examined to determine whether improvements can be made to streamline the flow of the patron through the library, perhaps reducing the number of service points as well as improving the efficiency of existing service points.

In lean manufacturing, such as at Toyota, a valuable tool used to analyze the production of a physical product is creating a flow diagram of how the product is transformed through various steps in the assembly process. A flow diagram can help identify areas where waste is added to the production process. In the TPS, sources for waste are outlined as the following eight areas (Liker, pp. 28–29):

1. *Overproduction*: The product is continuing to be manufactured even in the absence of any orders. This results in an accumulation of finished goods inventory. For libraries, overproduction may take the form of

librarians working on or creating subject or course guides that never get used by patrons or staff, along with the increasing number of these guides accumulating in the library's Web presence. In addition to never getting used by patrons, excess clutter, with too many similar or specific Web guides being displayed together, further diminishes the utility of using any individual resource guide.

2. *Waiting (time on hand)*: Employees wait around and do not do anything productive because of a number of factors. Such factors as automated processes that do not require manual interventions, machinery not operating because of missing parts, or employees idly waiting for the previous step in the manufacturing process to finish all result in an accumulation of work-in-process inventory in the workflow. In libraries, librarian or staff downtime may not be as important as in a manufacturing plant, but obvious areas where waiting occurs are circulation and reference services. Waiting at these service points may be caused by overstaffing at certain times, resulting in staff not having enough work to do. Are there activities and workflows in the library that exhibit diminishing returns? For example, adding more reference librarians at more service points and for longer time spans would likely show diminishing returns of performance. Are there ways that the library can modify existing reference services so that any additional time spent in reference increases the returns for the patron?

3. *Unnecessary transport or conveyance*: If the production workflow requires work-in-process inventory to be transported long distances or if incomplete products are moved to a storage facility, these can all introduce transport waste. For libraries, unnecessary transport of materials may occur in the technical services processing of physical books or other media. If the library requires a new book to be shipped to different facilities, that extra time and movement could be unnecessary and are good candidates to be reexamined for reduction of both waste in transporting materials and the time and effort required by library staff.

4. *Overprocessing or incorrect processing*: For the manufacturing of a product, this type of waste is a result of inefficient processes such as poor tool design for the job, incomplete or poorly thought out design specifications, or production of higher-quality goods (overprocessing) than are necessary. Libraries may spend too much time and effort processing their physical media or books through such areas as trying to find the

"perfect" call number of an item, while better use of valuable library staff time could be found.

5. *Excess inventory*: During the production of a product, inventory may accumulate at various stations in the assembly line, including the raw materials inventory, work-in-process inventory, and the finished goods inventory. While a small buffer is acceptable for lean manufacturers, the goal is to try to minimize the amount of goods at any one of the different stages in the process. For libraries, excess inventory could be in the number of copies in their bestseller collections. As demand for popular books or other media slowly declines, the library still maintains and even purchases new copies without considering the costs in terms of both purchasing price as well as the extra staff time needed to process those additional copies for the collection.

6. *Unnecessary movement*: Employees needing to move around and look for various tools to complete their work or needing to walk to a different location to finish their job are both sources of this type of waste. Libraries' circulation, reference help services, and technical services could all require librarians or staff to move too much to perform their tasks. For example, a process for a patron to check out a book may require a staff member to move through a number of different stations—check out the item in an integrated library system, desensitize a magnetic strip, and finally hand the material over to the patron; this could be reduced if the workstation's physical layout is more centralized and convenient for staff use.

7. *Defects*: If the parts being produced are defective, costs can quickly accumulate as the company repairs, rework, or scraps the defective product and takes other corrective action, such as producing replacements. Defects for libraries may be erroneous, outdated, or biased information provided by library staff to answer patrons' reference questions. When discovered, these errors erode the trust a patron has in the librarian's professional competency.

8. *Unused employee creativity*: If a company does not listen to or respect the ideas, comments, or skills of their employees, the company risks wasting their employees' potential. Library leadership not listening to and respecting the general staff and volunteers creates indifference, apathy, and even hostility among the staff that can easily translate to poor service to patrons. This unused creativity by library employees also is the source for simple improvements that together build a learning organization.

Toyota's strategy to improve the flow of manufactured automobiles through systematic reduction of the various types of waste listed above offers a compelling narrative and methodologies for libraries and library leadership to identify and minimize each of these eight waste sources.

3.8 KANBAN

When pull is preferred over push to improve the flow in a lean production system, there still needs to be a simple way to communicate with other participants that the inputs are needed in the current production process. This is done using an ingenious method developed by Toyota—a technology called **kanban**, which is simply translated as a "sign." In the most basic kanban setup, when an input runs low, a signal is sent to the supplier of that input that a small batch of the input is now required. The technology behind kanban is simple and usually does not require anything more sophisticated than physical flags made out of paper or plastic. Kanban systems can be more complex and tied to automatic, computer-based notification to upstream manufacturing stations that additional materials are needed for a specific station in the assembly line.

Rother and Shook's 1999 book about the TPS, called *Learning to See*, summarized Toyota's approach with the following phrase: "Flow where you can, pull where you must." Liker (p. 110) points out in his book *The Toyota Way* that, "The challenge is to develop a learning organization that will find ways to reduce the number of kanban and thereby reduce and finally eliminate the inventory buffer...kanban is something you strive to get rid of, not be proud of." Kanban is an inventory management tool with the goal of becoming lean by eliminating as much inventory as possible in the production process. Kanban is also a physical method and process that supports just-in-time delivery of products. The core idea behind kanban uses a signaling mechanism for alerting other stages in the manufacturing line that the inputs to the assembly line station are running low. This signal then creates demand for the upstream intermediary products or raw materials supplied from an external or internal source.

In the ideal pull-based manufacturing process, each product is reduced to a single-batch process, meaning that each station in the assembly line works on a single product at a time and does not continue until the demand for the item comes from the next station. In practice, single-batch manufacturing is not practical for many types of goods, so small-batch production is used by many lean manufacturing companies instead. In a small-batch production process, work-in-process inventory is allowed to accumulate until a small number of items are ready to meet the next station's demand. While small-batch production does introduce more work-in-process inventory, additional items in the batch provide an extra buffer in case of a slowdown or stoppage in other areas of the manufacturing process—a more likely occurrence in a lean manufacturing process. While eliminating buffers is one the goals of lean manufacturing, the implementation of lean processes—at least in the early stages—does involve the use of small buffers with kanban signaling when a station needs additional inventory or materials.

At the Tutt Library, a kanban system involving different colored paper slips has developed over time, mimicking the kanban small-batch approach even though the employees who intentionally designed the workflow did not have kanban in mind. When new material arrives in the library, in particular monographs or books, the physical items are delivered to the ordering department, paper slips are inserted into the books; these indicate both the priority and the type of processing that is needed. The rush-order items have a different colored paper slip than books that do not require any special handling. Any special notes or instructions are written on the paper slip as well. The new books are placed into a book cart and, when a sufficient number of books are included in a batch, the cart is moved to the stage in technical services (typically cataloging) that creates or copies a bibliographic record for the book, including assigning a call number. The final step adds a plastic cover and magnetic strip to the item before releasing it to circulation to shelve. If the item was a rush order, typically needed by a professor for a class or other coursework, the item is held by circulation, which then contacts the professor to inform them that the item is ready for pickup and use.

Other uses of kanban extend beyond the manufacturing and physical processing of inventory to using it in lean startup in software development. While physical flags signal to other downstream processes that the station requires more inventory, such a process is modified for the creation of intellectual assets such as software. The application of kanban as a scheduling tool for work in software development and related idea-driven organizations ensures that the work being completed is actually being driven by the requirements of or testing by the end users of the software or other intellectual or idea-heavy industry. For libraries, this application of kanban can be instituted for other projects that may not have actual physical artifacts but expand online resources or services.

3.9 THE ANDON SYSTEM IN LIBRARY WORKFLOWS

How can libraries increase the ingestion of physical and digital materials under their care while still maintaining an acceptable level of quality in cataloging and metadata? One approach is to adopt an idea from lean manufacturing, and more specifically TPS, that workers on an assembly line have access to a system called **andon**. With **andon**, if the worker observes a problem or fault in the production system, they activate a signal (typically a flashing light or sound) that alerts a team leader that there is a problem, but the assembly line keeps moving. If the team leader determines that there is an easy fix, then the assembly of the product continues on to the next station. If the problem is more severe, the entire production line is halted until the problem is resolved. The andon system is better suited for manufacturing and service workflows with short cycles, that are highly repetitive, and where help from other employees is available to immediately address the problem. While andon systems are highly developed and technically sophisticated in Toyota's automobile plants, the technology does not replace training and require employees to trust management's assurances that it is acceptable for employees to stop production if doing so brings to light problems in the manufacturing process.

As libraries' collections evolve and change, many use some form of batch processing to ingest large numbers of machine-readable cataloging (MARC) records into their catalog. A metadata **andon** system may be automated such that misspellings in titles, author names, and subject headings could be flagged and the cataloger alerted for manual intervention. Unlike a manufactured product, the quality of the metadata in bibliographic records can vary extensively. At one end of the spectrum, popular items have records that share most common metadata fields; these come from central source like Online Computer Library Center's (OCLC) WorldCat and are held by multiple libraries. At the other end of the quality spectrum, each metadata record in a batch load is unique, with few or no metadata shared with other records in the MARC record collection.

In the Catalog Pull Platform, MARC records provided by vendors are normalized to a predetermined standard set by the library. If during the normalization process errors occur, such as errors in the encoded Unicode titles or author names or invalid syntax, the script fails immediately and usually requires some intervention by either the cataloger or the developer. These errors are flagged and the process for that batch load does not continue until the error is corrected. In general, library technical services should care about the quality of records entering the library's catalog because these problems can surface later when library patrons and other users discover problems and errors when trying to use the library's catalog and services. A common and almost cliche reaction by library staff is when underlying problems in the quality of the source MARC records in a catalog surface when a new library discovery service is released. Misspellings, incorrect dates, wrong call numbers, or encoding errors that incorrectly identify the format or carrier media of a resource all are made more obvious in new environments that present a different view of the collection.

CHAPTER 4

Build–Measure–Learn as an OODA Loop

4.1 WHAT IS AN OODA LOOP?

In the 1950s and 1960s, John Boyd, an officer in the US Air Force, started designing the next generation of fighter jets like the F-16. In his analysis of how fighter pilots engage and respond in aerial dogfights with enemy pilots, Boyd realized that these pilots—and, after further study, organizations—typically go through four steps during a competitive or violent encounter: observe, orient, decide, and act, also known as the OODA loop (Figure 4.1). The faster an individual or an organization is able to cycle through this loop, the greater advantage they have over their opponents. By being able to respond more quickly to the changing environment and act, the individual or organization has a greater likelihood of success. The individual or organization with the more efficient and faster OODA loop tends to succeed over their opponents. This is not to say that the organization or individual with the faster OODA loop is always be the victor, because events and circumstances may favor another competitor with a slower OODA loop. The person or organization with the better OODA loop is, however, likely to be more successful over time in multiple conflicts.

The first stage of the OODA loop, **Observe**, occurs when an individual or organization initially encounters a situation. As the circumstances of the situation develop, the individual or organization, using outside or external information, along with what is happening during the interaction with the situation, filters key elements of the changing circumstances and then feeds these elements to the orientation stage of the OODA loop.

The second stage of the OODA loop, **Orient**, is when the observable elements of the **Observe** stage are placed into context within the perspective or understanding of the individual or organization. The context surrounding the situation is a result of a number of factors, such as the individual's or organization's cultural traditions and previous experience. The assumptions are analyzed and synthesized to create a hypothesis in the **Decide** step of the OODA loop.

Becoming a Lean Library
ISBN 978-1-84334-779-8

51

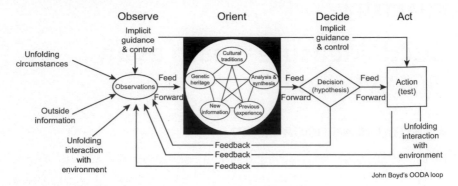

Figure 4.1 The OODA loop. *Source:* https://commons.wikimedia.org/wiki/File:OODA. Boyd.svg.

In the third stage of the OODA loop, **Decide**, the assumptions about the situation derived and created in the **Orient** step are pulled together into a hypothesis about the situation. This hypothesis includes probable outcomes for each of the different actions an individual or organization may take when responding to the conflict. In the **Decide** step, the best alternative among the possible actions is selected based on the previous **Observe** and **Orient** steps, moving the individual or organization toward the final step of the OODA loop.

In the forth and final stage, **Action**, the hypothesis from the **Decide** step is tested through the individual or organization actively participating in the situation and then responding to developments within the environment. In Boyd's classical formulation of the OODA loop, the **Action** step is immediately followed by the next iteration of the OODA loop with a new **Observe** step. This affects the changing circumstances along with the actions of the individual or organization. In a developing and fluid situation, the individual or organization may iterate through the OODA loop hundreds of times in a rapid succession as their opponent, following their own OODA loop, responds and adapts to the situation as well. The individual or organization can be "one step ahead" of their competitors if they can cycle through the OODA loop faster, and they will likely succeed because they are faster or more efficient than their opponents.

The OODA loop has proven to be useful in conceptualizing warfare, but there are detractors to Boyd's model, including members of the US armed forces. An OODA loop assumes that there are observable causes to known effects, while actual situations tend to more complex than a simple observable cause and effect. In the Iraq war that started in 2003, US Army officers—trained for decades in OODA techniques—spent too much time narrowing their focus of what to observe in anticipation of the orientation and decision steps of the OODA loop. This necessary filtering resulted in many of the armed forces attributing a relatively simple cause: the Iraq insurgency. To them, the insurgency was the result of mass layoffs of Baath party members. This simplistic cause ignored the more complex reasons individuals join the insurgency, such as Iraqi national pride (Lyle, 2011). If the observed causes of an event are different from the actual causes, then the orientation, decision, and action steps of the OODA loop will not create an effective response.

While libraries are not often involved in a life-or-death struggle over their existence, a lean startup approach encourages decision making and actions based on the library's observation of its operations and services. Instead of blindly making decisions about its collections or services without any references to its patrons, staff, or competitors, a library can systematically respond to change in a faster and more thoughtful manner with the active participation of the library's core constituents.

In his book on lean startups, Eric Ries (2011, p. 22) formulated a loop similar to Boyd's OODA loop, called build–measure–learn (BML). In Ries's BML loop, lean organizations go through an iterative process to improve the likelihood of success. Ries lists Boyd's work as an inspiration in formulating the BML loop as a simplified version of the OODA with a similar pattern (Ries, 2011). Each of these steps—build, measure, and learn—is examined in greater detail, with applications to libraries, in the subsequent sections of this chapter.

4.2 BUILDING FOR THE LOOP

In the build step of the BML loop, an organization builds a minimum viable product (MVP) to test the assumptions and marketability of the new service or technology. For the lean library, the build step of an MVP may involve partnering with a third-party vendor or external consultant for the actual construction of the resource or service. The build step could also be internally developed by librarians or staff, for example, newly digitized material from the library's special collections or a mobile app providing library hours. The actual software development may be a combination of internal and external partners, but the focus should be on getting the bare minimum of functionality implemented for the new product or services. One advantage of releasing an MVP early in the development process is that patrons and staff can start testing the product's functionality and usability early in its design.

The boundary between building something new and customizing an application for the institution's specific needs is blurry at best. More commercial and open-source services are offering an application programming interface (API)—a "data view"—with their services, using XML or JSON, to allow access to information about their resources. These APIs often provide methods or functions that a programmer can use to manipulate resources or services to integrate the service with the MVP even more. Within the lean library, it does not matter whether the service or resource was primarily developed in the library or is a mash-up of different products and services. The process of building an MVP is still the same: implement enough functionality for end users to test so that usage and adjustments to the product or service can be made based on the users' feedback.

Another consideration for a library when selecting technology to build an MVP is to what extent is the technology a pull platform or push platform. As explained briefly in the Introduction to this book and in further detail by Hagel, Brown, and Lang (Power of Pull, 76), pull platforms, such as popular and specialized social networks, have a number of characteristics that make the process of building an MVP easier. Pull platforms tend to offer more loosely coupled modules instead of a monolithic application. Large, complex enterprise software is a primary characteristic of more traditional integrated library systems. By being loosely coupled, contributors to a library's MVP are much more involved in its development, allowing for active participation as the user interacts with the MVP. A pull platform for a lean library typically includes more transparent code and is built with an API from the beginning of the product's development. However, in a blog post titled "The Lie of the API," Ruben Verborgh (2013), a PhD student at Ghent University, argues that a Web API service that requires a secret key and separate URLs for different data formats violates some of the basic assumptions of the Web, and that a better alternative are representational state transfer (REST) API Web services with content negotiation. When evaluating platforms, especially ones that are Web-based, a "REST-full" API is usually easier to use because a separate log-in or authentication is not necessary to use the API service. This may be one reason why the more popular pull platforms in use are open-source. Pull platforms tend to be enhanced and improved more frequently and fit extremely well with the lean startup philosophy of many iterative cycles of the BML loop.

Borrowing the example of Toyota, with its close relationships with critical suppliers in its production chain, libraries may be able to partner more closely with their library systems vendors when building an MVP. Most vendors offer trial periods for their products, and a BML modality can be adopted as a better alternative for the library's evaluation process. This trial period allows for a basic version of the vendor's product to be tested and used by the library's patrons. Giving immediate feedback to the vendor may not result in the problem being addressed, but it should provide a model or mechanism that encourages more of a lean approach to new products and services. This approach may not be possible with the vendors of longstanding library products (an integrated library system is one such product that comes immediately to mind); however, a new product or service is an opportunity to start implementing a more conscious BML loop with the library's new partner or supplier. This sort of partnership with a vendor in the development of an MVP requires a level of trust that is often absent in the relationships between libraries and their vendors, particularly if the vendors are still very much a "push"-oriented organization with top-down hierarchical structures. A lean library in pursuit of an MVP should encourage lateral collaboration of the library staff and librarians with the vendor's development and support staff.

In the **build** step, there are risks associated with building an MVP that have to do with setting unrealistic expectations and trying to include too much in the first-release product. There is a balance between providing enough functionality to give the individual using the MVP reason to do so without extending the development period for too long and including too many features. This shift in thinking requires educating targeted users about the initial value proposition of the MVP and the use of iterative BML cycles in the lean startup development model. There is, however, the danger of releasing an MVP too soon—one with nonexisting functionality and rough or sloppy design. If the MVP is too primitive, it risks alienating the end user; any improvements in subsequent MVP loops may be discounted or ignored because of the perceptions and experiences individuals had with the initial MVP.

Before moving to the **Measure** step, an important requirement for the MVP is the ability to capture the metrics that have been identified as being important. These measures signal that the MVP is addressing the problems or issues that are facing the end user. Ideally, the technology stack that the MVP is developed on allows these metrics to be captured, or it at least has some mechanism for data collection. This might be just the supporting Google Analytics or some other method for gathering these statistics. Some form of data gathering is a critical requirement in the next stage of the BML loop—that of the **Measure** step.

4.3 MEASURING DURING THE LOOP

Measuring interactions and tracking the usage of the MVP is the important second stage in the BML loop. By tracking the interactions users have with the product or service, the library can start testing its assumptions and hypotheses about how patrons or staff will use the product or service in the context of the larger project. Even for commercial products that the library is considering purchasing, a distinct measure step helps evaluate whether the product is meeting its intended purpose for the library.

For most libraries considering the purchase of a large commercial or third-party support contract for an open-source product, the company usually has a trial period to assist the library in evaluating the product or service. By being more mindful of and structuring the internal evaluation process as a single iteration of a BML loop, assumptions or marketing claims made about the product can be explicitly tested by the library's patrons or staff themselves. A downside of trying to use a BML loop during the trial period of a product is that the product being evaluated may not collect the metrics that would make testing these assumptions easier, or the vendor may refuse to release usage information to the library.

Measuring the process or flow of a user interacting with the MVP can be simple or complex. The library's focus should be on identifying those metrics that test the assumptions and hypotheses made in the build step of the loop. A critical requirement in the lean startup methodology is to make sure that an organization—in this case the library—can respond to actionable metrics while being on guard against the trap of vanity metrics. Vanity metrics are measurements that seem to indicate improvement but in fact measure the wrong processes or interactions and do little to track or test the underlying assumptions made by the library during the development of the MVP.

For example, the library may assume a high visitor count for a new Web-based resource is a valid metric for measuring popularity and usage. This can be problematic for a number of reasons, starting with how new visitors versus returning visitors are counted. If a daily count is taken, a visitor could be counted twice if they visit a Web page and then returns to the same page later the same day. A further complication is that merely visiting a Web page does not mean the visitor was successful in accomplishing their intended goal. For the commercial Web, an overreliance on using unique visitors versus actually per-user revenue can result in erroneous conclusions by the business that growth in visitor count is actually increasing the company's profitability. Likewise, a high visitor count for a new library Web property does not necessarily mean that the patron's information needs were being met by the service. A visually arresting design coupled with an advertising campaign by the library may result in increased visitor counts, but if the new design is not accomplishing its intended goal, then the library may not be measuring the correct attributes. Chapter 7 focuses specifically on this challenge of identifying and then measuring those attributes that are actionable metrics, instead of such attributes as visitor counts—or, in lean startup terminology, vanity metrics—that appeal to the ego but do not really deliver value to the library's leadership.

4.4 LEARNING FROM THE LOOP

The final step in the loop is analyzing the collected actionable metrics from the **Measure** step and learning from the data collected. A lean library uses these generated and captured metrics to test the hypotheses that were formalized in the **Build** step. This analysis identifies changes that should be made to the MVP before moving onto the next iteration of the BML loop. The goal of these measurements is to either affirm or refute the assumptions and hypothesis first made explicit in the **Build** step. Minor adjustments to the MVP may be all that are suggested by the analysis; or, the actionable metrics could warrant radical changes to the MVP. The difference from the first iteration of the BML loop is that assumptions and the hypothesis are adjusted based on the actionable metrics, and then the organization moves to the second iteration of the BML loop, starting again in the **Build** step for the product, resource, or service.

If your library is using a pull platform, changing and implementing any new functionality is a part of the organization's learning from and capturing the knowledge that develops from the previous steps in the loop. This knowledge helps individuals in the library apply the next round of hypothesis generation for future iterations through the **build, measure, learn** cycle. A pull platform should provide richer metric generation and management and storage of user activity that is occurring in the library's technology. After a complete iteration of the BML loop, a pull platform allows participants to receive rapid results from changes made in the build step. This quick response provides a creative space and opportunities for the library to innovate and take more risks in creating value for their patrons.

An additional challenge of the learn step in the BML loop is properly communicating the results of the **Measure** step to the library staff, library administration, and patrons. Library leadership must be able to illustrate clearly and distinctly how the attributes of the system or service being measured may need only minor tweaking or indicate a major overhaul is necessary. **Learning** is also about building a narrative of and a context for the changes, figuring out first what needs to be changed and, second, how those changes can be made in the next iteration of the BML loop. Communicating the results of the **Measure** step should be part of the **Learn** step because this sort of analysis and context is extremely helpful for extracting the tact knowledge of the users into a more explicit form that can be shared and built on for the next iteration of the BML loop for the project.

The importance of capturing a library's organizational memory in the **Learn** step is not just evaluating and critiquing the assumptions and hypotheses in the current loop but also being able to diffuse the knowledge being created in the BML loops to other areas and individuals in the library. Looking for ways that the lessons learned in the **build** and **measure** steps of the technology project, which may not be initially useful but could be valuable in other contexts, is a hallmark of a lean organization. Creativity is not just restricted to individuals coming up with totally new ideas, but includes empowered individuals who are able to remix and reapply existing structures and processes in novel ways in new contexts. By making an effort to capture and disseminate the learning that occurs during the learn step, libraries maximize the opportunities for creativity engagement among librarians, staff, and patrons.

Going back to the example of using a trial period for a commercial product or service as a modified BML iterative loop, a critical evaluation should be made to determine whether the vendor's claims are supported by the evidence collected in the measure step. If the vendor offers only a short trial period, then the lean library may be able to do only a single pass through the BML loop before needing to make a decision to purchase the vendor's product or not. Other reasons for using an abbreviated number of BML iterations for evaluating vendor products include minimizing staff time and efforts and to improve the bargaining position of the library in their negotiations with the vendor. If the product or service seems promising but is not currently supported by the testable claims made by the salespeople, one or two BML iterations while using the product should offer enough data that the library can use to either pursue purchasing the service, counteroffer with a reduced amount, or drop consideration of the product altogether.

Finally, the **learn** step of the BML loop informs the hypotheses in and direction of the next iteration of the product or project. With the confirmation or rejection of at least some of the initial hypotheses that led to the first **build** step, the lean organization is positioned for the next BML loop. Sometimes the metrics from the **measure** are inconclusive and do not provide sufficient evidence to either accept or reject the hypotheses from the **build** step. This should not be thought of as a failure in the BML process but as an indication that more work is needed to better define the question and examine the underlying assumptions in the project.

4.5 CATALOG PULL PLATFORM CASE STUDY: BML LOOPS

At Colorado College the academic year is broken up into eight 3.5-week "blocks"; students take a single class at a time for an intensive educational experience focusing on a single course. With this different model for the academic school year, the entire college's administrative and support activities revolve around the needs of students and faculty, who often do not have time to wait a couple of weeks for a resource or service, especially if it relates to the coursework in the current block. Meeting these student and faculty needs means that the library must be nimble and flexible. The structure of the block lends itself to projects and activities that align nicely with the short, iterative BML loops explained in this chapter. This is in contrast to a more traditional academic semester that lasts months, with students taking multiple classes during that time.

The first publicly released product of the Catalog Pull Platform is a catalog of Tutt Library's traditional monograph and serials collection using the library's bibliographic and authority MARC21 records. The TIGER catalog was initially based on a catalog designed by Aaron Schmidt of Influx Design. The TIGER catalog's front-end user interface was built using an open-source Web front-end framework called Twitter Bootstrap, along with jQuery and other javascript libraries.

The initial MVP of the TIGER catalog uses a semantic server, a Linked Data data store built with Elastic Search, MongoDB, and Redis. The semantic server (the source code repository is available at https://github.com/jermnelson/semantic-server) has a REST API as well as command-line utilities for ingesting and manipulating the MARC records. Initially, each MARC record was converted to JSON and then stored as JSON documents in MongoDB before being indexed into Solr for searching. The Redis piece in the semantic server is for capturing user and system metrics, along with data structures for caching, and supports the main user interface. Another difference in the TIGER catalog is that instead of making many roundtrips between the semantic data store and the Web front end, the user interface is loaded and then subsequent calls are made through AJAX calls to the semantic server REST API that dynamically loads the results into the user interface.

The first BML loop started with the release of the MVP TIGER catalog on March 3, 2014, and was completed on May 31, 2014. Other than recording individual reactions to the MVP, many features in the MVP were not implemented in the first iteration but were noted by people testing and reacting to the TIGER catalog. Some of these missing features were identified as good candidates for A/B testing in later BML iterations and are discussed at greater length in the case study in Chapter 7, *Actionable Metrics from Patron Activity*. One of these areas identified by people encountering the catalog was how to filter large result sets returned by a search. Although the mechanisms to filter these large sets in the back-end semantic store are the same, there are definitely a number of different ways to implement filter in the Web front-end user interface.

For the first iteration, enough minor bugs were identified in the MVP, along with the unsatisfactory performance of the auto-complete functionality for the search box and the need to provide a linked-data interface for the results and individual item display, that a longer interval was needed between the end of the first loop and the start of the second BML loop. In early April, a few bug fixes along with the addition of the entire collection of digital artifacts in Tutt Library's Fedora Commons digital repository, was publicly released for testing by and reactions from the community.

With the scarce human resources available to contribute to the Tutt Library Catalog, it took longer to analyze and interpret the results of the first BML loop. Because of the time and effort necessary to build the two filter components for A/B testing, other collaborators were sought out, and the beginnings of a community necessary for the Catalog Pull Platform to function as a pull platform was developed through presentations and attendance at a number of library and technology conferences. The new TIGER catalog for the library demonstrated the advantages of having an MVP—that while missing functionality that would be later implemented, it could be demonstrated and used in the critical incubation of the platform's early adopters.

Between the first and second BML loops, the catalog continued to be live, providing feedback and the chance to continuously release and integrate stable code into the MVP.

The second BML loop started in June 10 and was completed in August 30. While the first iterative BML loop was a reaction to and test of the initial design, the second BML loop focused on testing two different ways to filter large results set returned by the search index. The first design followed more a traditional library discovery layer approach and always displayed a box containing different facets that the patron could click to narrow the result set. For this BML loop, only three facets were offered: location in the library, year published, and the carrier format of the item. The second design used a dynamic, multilevel menu using the same three facets so that the patron could follow and select to filter the result set to more manageable number for review. To achieve the necessary number of catalog users to make any statistically significant outcomes or results, the A/B test for these two filtering design was run for a couple of months.

CHAPTER 5

Innovation Accounting and Francis Taylor

5.1 INNOVATION ACCOUNTING VERSUS FINANCIAL ACCOUNTING

Much of the success that organizations have in adopting lean startup principles is by using a different accounting approach called **Innovation Accounting**. Measuring the success or failure of a startup's product or service can be complex. In either cash-based or accrual accounting, revenues are recognized when a transaction occurs, and expenses either are recognized immediately or are amortized over a time period, with depreciation being calculated on a periodic basis. While these basic functions of accounting are still necessary and required in a lean startup or lean library, this approach fails to capture adequately the types of outcomes of interest to the lean startup. In a viable organization, innovation accounting holds the entrepreneurs or librarians accountable for their actions and decisions by tracking broader outcomes of an organization beyond it's revenue and expenses.

Innovation accounting is more responsive because it measures progress of the lean organization as attempts to meet milestones and prioritize the work (Ries, 2011, p. 8) For libraries, innovation accounting offers a mechanism for gathering and tracking metrics that extends beyond the library's budget. By measuring and responding to the outcomes that capture the value of the library, innovation accounting allows for more flexibility in prioritizing ongoing operations as the library strives to achieve its goals. For example, the value of an academic library on a college campus is often reduced to how much use—most broadly defined—the library achieves given it's current expenses. What the library budget and traditional accounting fail to capture is the value of the library's role in the intellectual life of the institution and the contribution of the library to the scholarship of the college's faculty and students. In innovation accounting, such contributions and value are made explicit and are used to drive the library's decisions as it develops into a learning organization.

As already iterated in previous chapters, the build–measure–learn loop for library projects is absolutely dependent on tracking, collecting, and

Becoming a Lean Library
ISBN 978-1-84334-779-8

63

analyzing data about a new service or resource. If the minimum viable product is accomplishing its intended purpose and is being used by the library's patrons, those metrics should feed into the innovation accounting process. Bootstrapping from preexisting accounting systems, the implementation of innovation accounting enriches the knowledge flows from libraries' operational workflows and processes.

5.2 KEY CONCEPTS OF INNOVATION ACCOUNTING

Embedded within a library's operations are a series of assumptions that need to be made more concrete and explicit. Together, these assumptions reflect the reality of the library's priorities and should be used in evaluating how well the library is meeting its goals and aspirations. Let us consider some examples from different libraries and see how these goals could be reformulated as an actionable metric in innovation accounting.

Three key concepts in innovation accounting build on one another:

1. **Establishing a baseline** of the library's operations through either current metrics or new reporting structures. If the library is trying to release a new technology-based service or resource—a minimum viable product, which was introduced earlier in Chapter 4—this baseline becomes even more important in demonstrating the value and relevancy of the new resource or service.

   The inputs to baseline include the library staff involved; external decision makers such as board members for public libraries and deans for academic libraries; and, most important, the library's patrons and potential patrons. Continued support for a new initiative often requires the library to demonstrate value to stakeholders sooner, and innovation accounting offers methods for accomplishing that task.

   The baseline for lean libraries is about creating hypotheses that test the assumptions behind the metrics. This process of creating testable hypotheses is explored in the next chapter, *Defining Hypotheses and Managing Complexity*.

2. From this baseline, the library makes **small, iterative changes** to shift the library from its current baseline toward the goal or ideal that was determined at the beginning of the process. These small changes are tracked frequently enough to improve the library's chances in accomplishing its goals. The risks associated with such incremental change can be minimized if the library is acting on the right metrics.

The focus of a lean startup's innovation accounting is on technology. This remains true for library technology projects, but the broader application of pull techniques and technology requires a different perspective on their application in a library. The users that will be affected by the project should be measured against the explicit goals of the project. If the process does not lend itself to these small, incremental changes, the problem may be because the project managers or library leadership are not directly involved in the process.

What should be the most important metric for lean libraries looking to make these changes—that of the actionable metrics of patron activity—is explored in detail in Chapter 7. With innovation accounting, small changes that improve the library patron's experience are tracked and analyzed, followed by incremental adjustments in the implementation of the project.

3. At critical junctions, innovation accounting provides feedback to the library decision makers about **determining the viability** of a project or service. If the library is embracing its learning mission, it should be able to pivot or persevere depending on the metrics being used to track progress. If the metrics do not support the current development or implementation path, the library can abandon unsupported activities while shifting limited resources to more promising avenues. The importance of this stage is such that is the main topic in Chapter 8.

These three elements of innovation accounting—**establishing a baseline; small, iterative changes;** and **determining viability**—are all ways innovation accounting can increase the organizational knowledge in a library. The nature of this knowledge has changed for libraries.

5.3 KNOWLEDGE STOCKS VERSUS KNOWLEDGE FLOWS

The definition of *knowledge* is fundamental to the philosophical specialty known as epistemology. This section does not try to provide a comprehensive or consistent description of knowledge, but instead focuses on how knowledge for lean libraries involves engagement between individuals and ideas and how those ideas are shared among individuals. Knowledge is not restricted to empirical observations but assumes some reflective qualities of individuals reasoning about their reality.

In the context of lean organizations and pull-based processes, knowledge can be broken down into two different kinds: tacit and explicit. Tacit knowledge, the knowledge that comes about through observation, training, and instruction from peers and experts, is a fruitful arena where knowledge is created and shared without much restriction. Explicit knowledge, which usually starts off as tacit knowledge that has been codified, tested, and more broadly shared, is typically the area where libraries concentrate their efforts. Tacit knowledge for libraries has meant specializing in collecting, curating, and managing physical material such as books, music, and motion pictures. Libraries must continue in this important task of creating explicit knowledge pools for their patrons. How can libraries encourage patrons to share and transfer their rich tacit knowledge into forms and structures that moves that tacit knowledge to more permanent explicit knowledge? At the boundaries between tacit and explicit knowledge is where engaged librarians of the future may dwell and excel at libraries' core mission of serving the information needs of their patrons.

For many, the library has been thought of as being merely a warehouse of books, and unfortunately this is still the case. This orientation and philosophy is very much consistent when libraries were the central repositories of explicit knowledge as well as physical items. It was easy to comprehend that these physical items were part of a larger collection of knowledge stocks—knowledge that is written, published, and acquired for the library's collections. With the library as the physical storehouse of knowledge stocks, patrons seeking information would have to come to the library, browse and search through the classification system using the card catalog, and finally find and check out the material from the stacks in the library. Direct applications of corporate management philosophies made increasing sense if books were thought of as an inventory and knowledge stocks were equivalent to manufacturing or distribution centers. The thinking was that library operations should be modeled on industry and books, the canonical representation of these knowledge stocks, could be treated as any other valuable commodity. When a library is a warehouse of books, the knowledge stocks are apparent and visible. In the world of information flows, where information is widely and cheaply available through the Internet, the role of the library as warehouse diminishes as patrons' information-seeking behavior changes to reflect this abundance of available information.

Increasing quantities of information are available through the Internet, including through Google Books, a result of Google's efforts in scanning the major monograph collections of a few large universities. Knowledge creation comes from more and varied sources, including nontraditional publishing platforms such as Twitter, blogs, or other pull publishing platforms, and the library must rethink its role in this new age of knowledge flows.

Instead of relying on an outmoded idea that a library's primary function is to manage a warehouse books, the library as an idea must be expanded. The library becomes a primary source of knowledge flow through its services and, more radically, through its digital curation and infrastructure support in the creation of patrons' knowledge and dissemination to larger regional communities and into the broader world.

Explicit knowledge flows is the realm of information and knowledge that librarians are most comfortable with because of centuries and generations of librarians managing their valuable resources: the physical manifestations of books, recorded culture, and general society. As gatekeepers, librarians focused on the transactional nature of the supply and demand of scarce information sources of these stores of explicit knowledge. To become a lean library, leadership must shift their perspective from that of managing an inventory of physical objects to a view that knowledge must be sought after, relationships developed, and value placed on the pursuit of sources of knowledge creation. The deep reservoirs of tacit knowledge that exist in a library's communities—its patrons and staff—should be the target and focus of future librarians.

As the authors note in the *Power of Pull*, "Trust is necessary because of the inevitable fumbling that occurs as we try to express and share tacit knowledge" (Hagel III, Brown, & Davison, 2010, p. 55). As librarians become more intimately involved in tacit knowledge creation within their communities, libraries have to continue to expand the level of trust that most people have in libraries and librarians. However, establishing and maintaining trust with patrons requires adjustments in how libraries approach and appear to their served communities. Librarians cannot continue to be the extreme introverts at the reference or research desk, deliberately trying to quiet the library's patrons over their noise.

Likewise, librarians should not become shallow salespersons with a superficial interest in the customer up until a sale is made or lost. Libraries have and need to continue to build long-term relationships with their patrons if they are to become this gateway or translator between the tacit and explicit knowledge flows of their communities.

The orientation and philosophy of the lean startup and lean manufacturing, coupled with the broader recognition and development of pull-based systems, have created an opportunity for libraries to become much more active at the boundaries between tacit and explicit knowledge flows. Libraries, as publishers and repositories of the creative and intellectual artifacts of communities, are poised to offer the types of services and resources that are responsive to their patrons—first creating tacit knowledge relevant to their current situation and circumstances and then being able to describe, record, and transfer this knowledge to other individuals in the community and broader world.

This move from tacit to explicit knowledge starts within the library itself. A key concept from innovation accounting is the establishment of a library's baseline, part of which is looking at all of the different areas within a library's operations and services and pointing to where staff have developed over time a large reservoir of tacit knowledge about their particular responsibilities. The features, or the stories behind the work being done by library staff, other employees, and volunteers, need to integrated into the broader tapestry of information and data that make up the nature and reality of the library's state at a moment in time; this is discussed next.

5.4 FRANCIS TAYLOR AND THE LIBRARY'S BASELINE

Unlike a startup, most libraries are established, long-running institutions that already offer rich sources of data being generated from their day-to-day operations. Many times, the workflows and processes of daily library operations were designed and implemented using variations of and theories from scientific management. Scientific management was first popularized in the late nineteenth and early twentieth centuries by Francis Taylor. An American business theorist, Taylor believed that by breaking down a typical work process into smaller parts or tasks, those parts could be optimized by reducing the time needed to accomplish the task.

As Francis Taylor's ideas and processes, codified into what is now referred to as scientific management, become more dominant, industrial engineers flooded various manufacturing enterprises, measuring both time to completion of a task and the steps in the physical processes to do so. As these industrial engineers documented the work being done by employees, those employees who shared their knowledge of time-saving techniques and quality improvement quickly discovered that because of their contributions, they were now expected to produce more products at a higher volume than before. This eventually created an antagonistic relationship between the industrial engineers and the employees, whereby employees refused to share their labor-saving ideas and techniques, even going as far as slowing down if the employee was being observed by an industrial engineer and refusing to participate in further studies. As a result, extensive bureaucracies developed with hierarchical controls and extensive rules and rigid regulations for controlling the labor force.

Libraries, especially larger academic and public ones, have over time grown large bureaucracies that share many of the characteristics of Taylor-designed organizations. Adler (1998), a researcher who has extensively studied organizational structures, identified two types of bureaucracies: coercive verses enabling. While on the surface it may be difficult to distinguish the two, the key difference is that an enabling bureaucracy is focused on empowering the individual to be a decision maker and be active in the implementation and use of the rules. Unlike a coercive bureaucracy, an enabling bureaucracy focuses on best practices that can be modified based on both the performance of the employee and the productive result or outcome of the work. By contrast, in a coercive bureaucracy employees are evaluated against performance standards that filter out poor performance, without much recourse for the employee to change or alter those top-down performance standards. Adler (1998, p. 4), reacting to a corporate fad in the late 1990s of wholesale reduction of bureaucratic layers, observed that, "Reducing the number of layers, procedures, and staff may be necessary in some cases, but most managers recognize at the same time that large-scale, complex organizations need some hierarchical structure, some formalized procedures, and some staff expertise."

The development of the Toyota Production System by Toyota Motors started by engineers and executives observing and documenting how Ford Motor Company used Francis Taylor's concepts to design employees' workstations in an assembly line. Ford, and other adopters of Francis Taylor's ideas, looked to optimize each activity that added valued to the product. In addition to applying such observations to each of the value-added steps in a production process, Toyota just as rigorously applied the same attention and effort to all non–value-adding steps (i.e., what was considered wasted) in the manufacturing process. Under the Taylor model, a traditional manufacturer's main focus is increasing the throughput of the assembly line without regard for the demand for the product. This results in large work-in-process and finished goods inventories. Because the incentive of factory managers is to keep production running regardless of any problems, the quality of the goods being manufactured can suffer at any one of the assembly line's workstations. Any mechanical failure in the production line's machines is extremely costly, so employees are less likely to stop the assembly line when a quality problem does occur.

Although Toyota exemplifies an enabling bureaucracy, with both automated and manual controls in place that superficially resemble a Taylor-inspired model, employees at Toyota still operate under tight timelines and production quotas. Unlike a coercive bureaucracy, employees are encouraged to actively seek out ways to improve production processes and standards. From the time they start at Toyota, engineers are expected to learn and use extensive design checklists for every aspect of a new car. These design checklists are not static, but are added to and modified based on the specific needs for a particular automotive design. These checklists offer standards that must be met and help normalize practices and procedures across Toyota. By noting each source of data from library operations, a similar checklist for creating an initial library baseline should be used for any future snapshots of library operations.

As Liker (2004, p. 147) points out in *The Toyota Way*, the difference between a coercive and enabling bureaucracy at Toyota is in how those standards are written and who contributes to them. If the standards are too rigid and inflexible, employees will not contribute more than what is required for the task at hand, even if the employees' ideas and creativity could improve those standards. On the other hand, if the standards are not defined well, performance, quality, and cost metrics can suffer as a result. Striking a good balance between the two includes making the standards specific enough to be useful guides while still being flexible to accommodate exceptions and unique circumstances that may come up. In addition, those workers who are implementing the standards need to be able to participate and improve those standards based on the actual practice and outcomes of the work process.

Moving forward to the present, employees' actions and time are continually monitored by employers through computers and extensive sensor networks. While such monitoring of employee work habits and products would be a dream for yesteryear's industrial engineers following Francis Taylor's models, in the past employees blindly focused on one or two metrics, such as production output, while ignoring other equally important aspects, like the total quality of the end product. A modern application of Francis Taylor's techniques tries to improve existing workflows through increased capturing and analysis of metrics, known as "big data."

Big data is promoted as a way to increase the productivity and efficiency of an organization's goods, services, and people. The promise of big data is that the patterns and trends that are difficult to observe or are not apparent can be teased out of the operations and used for continual improvement and feedback to individuals responsible for the workflow. The key difference between an enabling and coercive bureaucracy in a big data context is if the front-line individuals are active participants in the collection and interpretation of the data they collect, or if they are powerless pawns in management's imposed policies and coercive technologies.

Libraries have also used Francis Taylor's principles to design material processing, circulation, and system designs. Starting in the 1950s and 1960s, all types and sizes of libraries adopted or attempted to adopt Taylor's methods for improving functions related to the physical processing of material (Dougherty & Heinritz, 1966) Other areas of a library's operations that were heavily influenced by Taylor include circulation activities such as lending material to patrons and a library's efforts to recover late or damaged material. These and other Taylor inspired library work processes do generate performance data, particularly about quantity or other transaction-based metrics, and can be used in a general survey of a library's operations as well as helping in establishing a library's operational baseline.

Instead of trying to start from scratch by collecting, measuring, or estimating a library's current operations, adapting and building on Taylor-influenced workflows in a library offers one mechanism for establishing a library's baseline. While Francis Taylor's focus was on improvements to specific tasks that had been deconstructed from larger workflows, such measurements and data collection can easily be repurposed by a lean library into better estimates of its baseline. However, overreliance on the statistics generated from these existing work processes can miss significant aspects of the library's operations. Just like how Toyota extended the Taylor-inspired assembly line designs of Ford into a broader examination of not only production quantity but also gaps and the nonproductive steps and waste, so too does a library interested in creating an accurate and comprehensive baseline need to consider how to capture metrics around all of the various workflows and service points in its operations.

What do some of those nonproductive steps look like? Returning to the circulation processes mentioned in Chapter 3, nonproductive steps that are not captured include such efforts as library patrons first discovering and then locating a book on the library's shelves. The success or failure of the patron in finding material is not being captured, but some indication or data proxy should be included in the library's baseline. The library's circulation functions start when initiated by the patron and are tracked by the library's operations through the entire process, through the patron leaving the library with the book. With the current setup, most circulation functions in a library center around the physical management of its inventory; this then lends itself to type of analysis favored by Francis Taylor and by lean manufacturers like Toyota. Other service points in the library, including reference and online Web resources, can be included when searching for nonproductive steps in the entire flow of patrons' discovery and access of materials.

5.5 ACCOUNTING FOR INTRALIBRARY LOAN USING THE JUST-IN-TIME PRINCIPLE

A critical characteristic of the Toyota Production System is the adoption of the Just-In-Time (JIT) principle. JIT is the idea that tools, processes, and techniques should be modified so that a company can produce and deliver a customized product for the customer with a short lead time and in small quantities (Liker, 2004, p. 23). Reformulated or tweaked, JIT principles are already present in many of the core activities in a library. Resource sharing, or intralibrary loan (ILL), is a JIT process. In the vast majority of cases, resource sharing is driven by the service demand of patrons requesting a resource that the library does not own. The item can be retrieved from other participating libraries in local, regional, or national ILL services. An incoming ILL request to a library is driven again by a request by a user–in this case, a remote user of another library. Both fulfillment and request for resources by a library patron in a typical ILL operation are demand-driven services offered by the library.

In academic libraries, resource sharing correlates with the academic calendar. Requests and fulfillments peak before final examinations at the academic institution, when student's research papers become due. For public libraries, demand for materials may not vary as much in academic libraries, but demand may be driven by other factors. A book becoming popular because of a new release, word of mouth, social networks, or the release of a new motion picture adapted from a book or older movie may increase the demand for a library's materials and resources. Because of resource-lending agreements between academic and public libraries, this demand can be smoothed out and shifted between libraries. With the variable demand for ILL services, libraries accept that there will down time when resource-sharing activity is minimal, whereas at other times resource sharing is active.

These ILL requests are usually tracked, collected, and recorded as the primary metrics used for evaluating the resource-sharing activity of a library. Breaking down the activity further, libraries' record-related statistics include the number of outstanding incoming and outgoing requests not fulfilled, the amount of time required to fulfill an incoming request, and the total number of requests by the library's patrons. These statistics are usually generated quarterly, semiannually, or annually; any significant changes in resource-sharing activity are not discovered until then.

Adopting innovation accounting for the ILL service increases the frequency with which these metrics are generated— as often as a daily process or in real time, depending on the capabilities of the library's technology. Generating these statistics frequently gives the library the flexibility to find and address much sooner any problems that are occurring. For example, if the fulfillment time for an incoming request increases suddenly, the library can isolate and find out what is causing this delay. Another benefit of increasing the frequency of data collection and analysis is that, following a lean methodology, small changes to improve ILL services can be tracked more quickly and used in an iterative fashion to make further changes. The resource-sharing service, even if it is currently operating to the satisfaction of the library's administration, likely has points that could be improved, perhaps by increasing the quality of the fulfillment service, decreasing the amount of time it takes for an ILL request to be completed, or eliminating specific steps in the process.

Libraries rightfully boast about their traffic and usual increase in requests and fulfillment in their resource-sharing operations as evidence of the library's utility to the communities they serve. Building into resource-sharing operations better metric gathering can also encourage ILL staff to identify and suggest changes as active and empowered agents in their own work. This an important area of library services that can be improved and strengthened for print and other physical media, even if the overall demand by patrons may be decreasing because of the shift in libraries' collections to digital journals and books. This shift in collection development from physical to digital is of concern to the library's role in resource sharing, especially when considering the barriers to loaning imposed by restrictive copyright conditions implemented by electronic resource publishers and enforced through various digital rights management (DRM) technologies. So far, there has not been a equitable market solution; these DRM and copyright restrictions constrain how a library can share its collections while still adequately compensating the authors and publishers for their efforts.

5.6 CATALOG PULL PLATFORM CASE STUDY: ESTABLISHING TUTT LIBRARY'S BASELINE

An explicit pull source in the Catalog Pull Platform, as mentioned in Chapter 2, is the various reporting and functionality requirements of institutions inside and outside the library. While metrics are easily collected through the platform, creating a baseline for operations at the Tutt Library is a continuing challenge. Using existing sources of quantitative and qualitative metrics that the library is already collecting, these metrics were initially entered into the Catalog Pull Platform's semantic server. Subsequent to that initial data load, automated workflows that channeled data that originated outside the Catalog Pull Platform into the semantic server. Connectors were built, often using vendor-provided application programming interfaces, to pull these data sources into the semantic server for further manipulation.

The major data sources for calculating Tutt Library's initial baseline include the following:

- Legacy Integrated Library System (ILS)

  The Tutt Library's legacy ILS, the Millennium product from III, was first purchased in the mid-1990s; over the subsequent years, the library has upgraded its version to keep up with the latest releases. In 2012 the library started discussing migrating the ILS to a vendor-hosted version, and the final decision was made and implemented in 2013. Reporting and generating statistics in Millennium was relatively easy for some data points but was difficult or impossible for others needed by institutions associated with the Tutt Library.

  The ILS is the primary source for circulation statistics such as total number of checkouts during the year, what items circulated the most, and the average number of checkouts for each monograph in the collection. The legacy ILS is also used for calculating the total number of items added to each collection, the distribution of different formats in the library's collection, and the average age of items across the different collections in the library.

  In the first iterations of the Catalog Pull Platform's semantic server, the machine-readable catalog (MARC) 21 bibliographic records were converted from MARC21 to a JSON-format document that was then inserted into the MongoDB MARC database. These MARC JSON document includes the identity of each item record attached to the bibliographic record in Millennium. Using an XML interface into Millennium based on the item number, real-time usage statistics, such as date of last check-in, total number of checkouts, and total renewals, could be harvested.

- Google Analytics

  The use of Google Analytics in the library is a topic discussed in Chapter 6, but for the purpose of establishing a library baseline, Google

Analytics is a useful source of demographic and usage statistics for those Web properties and resources purchased or supported by the library. While Google Analytics is being used with the Tutt Library's Millennium catalog, this service from Google is also used on the library's Web site, its library's Django-based discovery layer, and Islandora with the Fedora Commons digital repository. The Tutt Library rarely uses the more advanced features of Google Analytics, such as determining click-through rate and other more commercial-oriented metrics.

- LibGuides

The Tutt Library has been using a couple of products sold by Springshare, the most notable of which is their LibGuides product. LibGuides allows librarians and library staff to create research guides for a number of broad topics organized by alphabet, subject area, and course. LibGuides also were created for more specific topics and not just restricted to academic subject of interest to Colorado College students. Librarians created LibGuides for the college's faculty and staff on such topics as long-term care insurance being offered at a discount by the college, and for National Poetry Month. Some questions were asked regarding the use and utility of these LibGuides for the primary focus of undergraduate education by the library, especially when there is almost no activity for the majority of the LibGuides. The ease of creating and sharing content between librarians at Colorado College, as well as library LibGuides from libraries across the country, continued support for LibGuides among the library's staff and patrons.

- Reference and instruction

Initially, Tutt Library's reference statistics were collected through a custom Hypertext Preprocessor (PHP) and MySQL application that stored manually entered information on librarians' interactions with patrons at the Tutt Library's reference help desk, over the telephone, using online chat, and through office reference interviews. This application lasted over 5 years, but a replacement was needed when the college's and library's Web sites were migrated to a new content management system that was incompatible with the old PHP Web server. Tutt Library instruction statistics were gathered a number of different ways, including paper forms and online surveys through SurveyMonkey. With the need to replace the PHP application, the library decided to subscribe to LibStats, a library statistical product from Springshare, the same company responsible for LibGuides.

The establishment of Tutt Library's baseline involved multiple sources of data from various purchased, open-source, cloud-hosted platforms, as well as Colorado College's information technology system's virtual machine infrastructure. Building and explaining how these sources of data involve shifting from static knowledge stocks to knowledge flows of information drives how Tutt Library builds a compelling narrative.

CHAPTER 6

Defining Hypothesis and Managing Complexity

6.1 WHAT IS A HYPOTHESIS?

When asked, many individuals are able to give a reasonable definition of hypothesis. A hypothesis is a way to model assumptions about the reality of a situation that can then provide predictions to be tested. A hypothesis is made up of one or more related statements about a situation or circumstance, and each statement can be falsifiable, or disproved. Experiments can be constructed that attempt to confirm or deny the "truthfulness" or correctness of a hypothesis's assumptions. The "correctness" of a statement in the hypothesis either is deductively confirmed or is calculated from a statistical analysis of observations during the experiments. Another core characteristic of a well-formed and correct hypothesis is that any experiments to test the hypothesis can be independently collaborated and replicated, although in practice, replicating experiments is not as common among working scientists.

Spivak (2013, p. 7) describes the scientific method as:

A hypothesis analyzed by a person produces a prediction, which motivates the specification of an experiment, which when executed results in an observation, which analyzed by a person yields a hypothesis.

A third way to evaluate a hypothesis has recently received much interest and work, that is, automatically generating associations and behavioral predications using distributed and parallel machine learning algorithms that compute deep statistical analysis and modeling from data sets generated by mechanical, physical, biological, or behavioral means. More a marketing term, "Big Data" is often how these types of analysis allow for hypothesis testing; the popular and trade press refer to the use of large data sets. A legitimate counterargument could be made that this third way of conducting scientific inquiry is really just a special case of the empirical method that has been used with great success over the past four centuries or so. Another looming issue in "Big Data" is the ability to replicate experiments (or more the lack of this). If the outcomes and validation of a hypothesis are reliant on a specific data set and that data set cannot be replicated, these methods

Becoming a Lean Library
ISBN 978-1-84334-779-8

lack the critical characteristic of independent replication, or being testable using the scientific method.

In the harder sciences, such as physics and chemistry, experiments and the conclusions that can be drawn about the correctness of the hypothesis are considered to be more rigorous than those in other academic fields. In economics and related disciplines such as sociology or political science, experiments that can generate the type of rigorous validation or rejection of a hypothesis that is a characteristic of fields such as experimental physics are much more difficult, if not impossible, to design.

Library and information science falls into the less rigorous and less empirical end of the social sciences spectrum. Proving or disproving hypotheses is harder in library and information science than in other fields. Hypotheses creation and testing in libraries first came about in analyzing work processes and flows in libraries' technical services. In technical services, unlike other library service points such as reference, data are easily collected and analyzed, making hypothesis creation easier. Statements of belief can be tested directly, either through experimental design or through continued data collection of the workflow processes.

For example, a manager may believe that, in an existing library acquisition workflow, eliminating a step of visual confirmation that the call number on a book's spine label is correct and matches in the book's machine-readable catalog (MARC) record for new printed material would not materially affect patrons while improving the speed with which the department can process new material. Data to confirm or deny this hypothesis would be generated and evaluated from two sources: the number of complaints from patrons reported by the public services points that could be directly attributed to the incorrect call number on a book, as well as the number of items that are processed through technical services.

The problem of inaccurate conclusions being drawn from the data collected by the library stems from a much more general issue. Capturing and understanding patrons' data can be complex and difficult, so using negative indicators (such as problems with wrong call numbers reported by public patrons) to positively assert the hypothesis that a visual confirmation of a book's call number is not needed may fail to accurately reflect patrons' experiences in the library. Skipping a visual quality control may not affect the patrons, but this hypothesis underestimates the problems of assessing patrons' activity if the only measurement is reported patron complaints.

A hypothesis created with implicit and explicit assumptions about the online search and interaction behavior of patrons allows for better tracking and measurement, and it is the core impact on the learning organization's analysis of the usage and interactions of the patrons using the library's online services. An important caveat is the practice of indiscriminate collection and retention of patron usage data. Without ensuring proper security and that privacy controls are in place for respecting individual privacy, data about patrons can be misused or, even worse, become a security risk from criminal actors. The library profession's long tradition of protecting patron activity should mean that libraries are extra vigilant in protecting the online activity of patrons and their use of the library's physical resources and services. Most vendors and even nonprofit organizations engage in detailed tracking of their users' activity. Libraries and library technology should not just blindly adopt these practices, but actively create and test them to ensure that the libraries are upholding the values and traditions of protecting a patron's privacy in the usage of library resources and services.

To help libraries become better online citizens, library leadership should consider being more communicative about the collection, retention, and use of identifiable patron data in the library's technical infrastructure. The library may not be able to prevent third parties—be they library technology vendors or publishers of databases of electronic content—from collecting data about patrons who use these technology services. Libraries can, at a minimum, collect and publish the privacy policies of these third parties and design systems that require patrons to "opt in" on any collection of personally identifiable data. The library should also be explicit about how it uses patron information that is not personally identifiable. While the methods and processes of a lean library do encourage the collection and retention of data, particularly in the build–measure–learn loop, libraries should also be mindful and transparent about the reasons why such data are being collected, how long the data will be retained, and what impacts, if any, such data storage and management will have for the individual patron.

6.2 BUSINESS MODEL CANVAS

In his 2013 article in the *Harvard Business Journal* titled, "Why the Lean Start-Up Changes Everything," Steve Blank outlines nine components of a single-page business model canvas to help startups define their hypothesis and aid in analyzing their business partners (Figure 6.1). The lean business model canvas is an adaptation of Alex Osterwalder's original single-page business model but is more actionable and entrepreneur-focused (Maurya, 2012). Regardless of the structure of the business model canvas, this technique allows new startups, existing businesses, and established institutions to capture what is important and what the organization is trying to do in

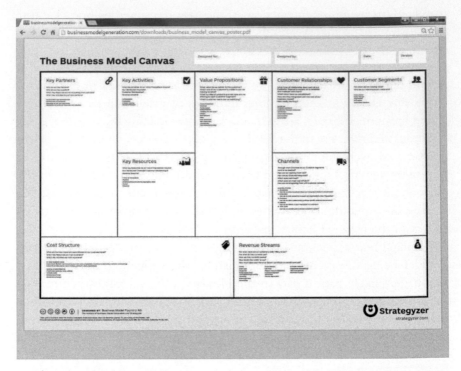

Figure 6.1 Template of the business model canvas. *From the Strategyzer website,* http://businessmodelgeneration.com.

single page. While libraries rarely (if ever) need to pitch a business plan to investors or customers, the business model canvas gives a library a way to communicate with important stakeholders, including college administration, library boards, library staff, volunteers, and anyone with an interest in the library about the relationships, services, and resources in the library.

For libraries, Osterwalder's original business model canvas offers a way to describe the value proposition of a library broken down into nine areas that need modifications to reflect the usually nonprofit status of the library. To illustrate these concepts, this and the next section use a fictitious medium-sized suburban library branch and create a business model canvas using Osterwalder's origin design. When finished, the business model canvas is used as the starting assumptions for hypothesis generation and testing later in the chapter.

6.2.1 Key Partners

The first area or box on the business model canvas is a listing of **key partners** for the library. While these partners vary depending on the

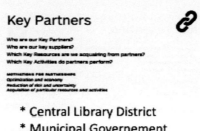

Key Partners

Who are our Key Partners?
Who are our key suppliers?
Which Key Resources are we acquiring from partners?
Which Key Activities do partners perform?

MOTIVATIONS FOR PARTNERSHIPS
Optimization and economy
Reduction of risk and uncertainty
Acquisition of particular resources and activities

* Central Library District
* Municipal Governement
* Community Volunteers
* Local Newspaper &
  Community Bloggers

Figure 6.2 Key partners for suburban branch library.

type, size, history, and location of the library, identifying and listing these critical partners helps to place the library within the larger context of its community.

For the fictitious suburban branch library, the **key partners** would be the central library district, the local municipal government, and community volunteers (Figure 6.2). One **key partner** that should not be overlooked is the local media, including newspapers, television shows, and community bloggers.

6.2.2 Key Activities

As libraries adapt to and change in response to the large shifts in how people find, consume, and create media and, more broadly, information, the **key activities** that are associated with libraries need to reflect the library's new roles as creation spaces and publishers. However, the library's traditional activities should not be ignored or abandoned, but modified to reflect these new realities. Other **key activities** of the library include information literacy instruction and reference help for patrons.

In the example pubic library, the **key activities** would be the circulation of books, magazines, and video media. Intralibrary loan, reference, and Internet access are all other **key activities** of the library within its community (Figure 6.3).

6.2.3 Key Resources

In the past, libraries were the primary source for the reference, learning, and pleasure reading material needs of their communities. While these various collections were the central focus of libraries' workflows such as technical

Key Activities

What Key Activities do our Value Propositions require?
Our Distribution Channels?
Customer Relationships?
Revenue streams?

CATEGORIES
Production
Problem Solving
Platform/Network

* Circulation of books, magazines,
  and video media
* Intra-library loan
* Reference services
* Internet access

Figure 6.3 Key activities for suburban branch library.

Key Resources

What Key Resources do our Value Propositions require?
Our Distribution Channels? Customer Relationships?
Revenue Streams?

TYPES OF RESOURCES
Physical
Intellectual (brand patents, copyrights, data)
Human
Financial

* Library Staff
* Popular Collections
* Unique special collections
* Unique digital artifacts

Figure 6.4 Key resources for suburban branch library.

services, circulation, and acquisitions, libraries' **key resources** have shifted in the past decade or so with the exponential growth in the availability of electronically accessed resources; the purchase and provision of these by libraries has become more important. While libraries—in particular special collections and archives—have usually collected material of interest, such as local ephemera and biographies, they have just started to tentatively collect electronic artifacts of their communities in an effort to collect these **key resources** for their digital archives. As cliche as it sounds, however, the most important **key resource** for any library is the people working for and using the library.

For the example public library, the **key resources** are the library staff coupled with the most used collections (Figure 6.4). In this medium-size public library, the most used collections include bestseller fiction, popular DVDs, and children books.

6.2.4 Cost Structure

Most libraries' **cost structure** is made up of three main areas: staff costs, collection costs, and infrastructure costs. Staff costs for libraries are usually stable, with minimal variation from year to year. Collection costs, however, vary widely, with static or even declining budgets for printed books and journals but escalating and increasing costs for electronic journals and other online resources. While it is encouraging to hear about libraries that successfully lobbied for a municipal tax increase to build a new library or accomplished successfully fundraiser campaign for a new academic library on a college campus, libraries in general are usually located in aging buildings with worn-down infrastructure. Infrastructure expenses beyond keeping the library structurally sound, such as new computers, wireless networking, or furniture, are additional costs that can be postponed for only so long before patrons' demands are no longer being met.

For libraries with large legacy organizations, the **cost structures** and budgets can be stratified, with considerable resistance by librarians and library staff to changing the status quo. In the example public library, the cost structure would be similar to any organization of that size, with staff, collections, and infrastructure making up the major costs to the library (Figure 6.5).

6.2.5 Value Propositions

Libraries need to periodically ask the question, "What value are we delivering to patrons?" The Pew Research Center's 2013 survey of American public libraries lists four areas where high percentages of Americans feel public libraries are **value propositions** to their communities. Over 95% feel that libraries gives everyone a chance to succeed and that libraries promote literacy in their communities. Also, over 80% of those surveyed believe that public libraries provide services that the community would have difficulty finding alternatives for, and over 94% think that public libraries improve the quality of life in their communities (Zickur, Rainie, & Purcell, 2013) (Figure 6.6).

Cost Structure

What are the most important costs inherent in our business model?
Which Key Resources are most expensive?
Which Key Activities are most expensive?

IS YOUR BUSINESS MORE
Cost Driven (leanest cost structure, low price value proposition, maximum automation, extensive outsourcing)
Value Driven (focused on value creation, premium value proposition)

SAMPLE CHARACTERISTICS
Fixed Costs (salaries, rents, utilities)
Variable costs
Economies of scale
Economies of scope

* Library staff salaries and benefits
* Print and Electronic Collections
* Physical infrastructure of library building
* Computer workstations and networking

Figure 6.5 Cost structure for suburban branch library.

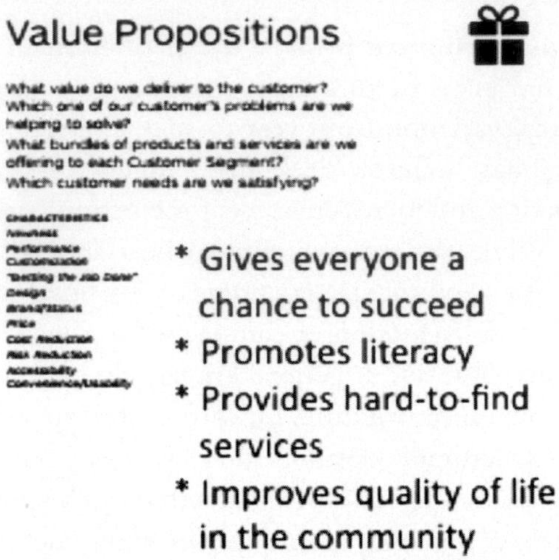

Value Propositions

What value do we deliver to the customer?
Which one of our customer's problems are we
helping to solve?
What bundles of products and services are we
offering to each Customer Segment?
Which customer needs are we satisfying?

CHARACTERISTICS
Newness
Performance
Customization
"Getting the Job Done"
Design
Brand/Status
Price
Cost Reduction
Risk Reduction
Accessibility
Convenience/Usability

* Gives everyone a
  chance to succeed
* Promotes literacy
* Provides hard-to-find
  services
* Improves quality of life
  in the community

Figure 6.6 Value propositions for a suburban branch library.

In the example library, the **value propositions** of this specific branch do not differ much from the four areas identified in the Pew survey. As a community good that provides opportunities and services for all members of the community while promoting literacy and the quality of life, the local library branch does offer value that would be difficult, if not impossible, to find an acceptable replacement for. The library's value to all segments of the community, including those individuals who are financially unstable, are without work, or are underemployed, cannot be completely captured.

6.2.6 Customer Segments

For libraries, classifying their patrons into different segments and then building collections to meet these **customer segments**' needs has a long historical precedent. For public libraries, adult learners and children are important cohorts whose needs are identified and services programmed and budgeted for. For academic libraries, **customer segments** are the institution's faculty, students, and staff along with public scholars who wish to use the libraries' collections. While these categories are very broad, we go into much more detail about the process of deconstructing these broad categories into patron cohorts in Chapter 7.

For the medium-sized branch library, the adult and children patron cohorts can be further broken down by specific **customer segments** such as retirement, unemployment, age, reading ability, and income (Figure 6.7).

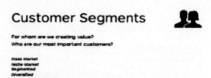

Customer Segments

For whom are we creating value?
Who are our most important customers?

Mass Market
Niche Market
Segmented
Diversified
Multi-sided Platform

* Adult patron
* Child patron
* Retired patrons
* Unemployed patrons

Figure 6.7 Customer segments for suburban branch library.

6.2.7 Customer Relationships

For each of the different **customer segments** identified in the last section, the library has a **customer relationship** that is tailored to that segment. With libraries' limited resources and staffing, they try to meet some of the most important information needs of each cohort. In public libraries, adult learners may require more one-on-one reference help to navigate and utilize the library's catalog and to find relevant material in the library's collections. Child services by the public library, such as summer reading programs, attempt to establish a positive relationship that continues over the lifetime of these young patrons. In academic libraries, the research and instruction help for first-year students is built upon in each subsequent year.

Anecdotally, students require research and reference help in their first year at college, particularly at 4-year institutions, but the library's service points do not see the student again until the student's senior year when he or she is researching and writing a final thesis or senior final project. Therefore it is very important for the library to establish at least a positive impression on the student so that he or she is more likely to use the library in their later years. Academic libraries also need to be able to offer research assistance and a strong lending program for their institution's faculty and staff.

Libraries typically do not track expenses by their patron cohorts, so libraries do not know whether any particular cohort costs significantly more in terms of staff time or resource requirements. This information would be valuable for a library in deciding how to allocate future resources and staffing. If expenses are broken down by customer segments, the library may discover that some cohorts are costing the library too much at the current level of funding and staffing, to the detriment of other library cohorts. Even if the library does not change their operations, knowing the costs of supporting each library patron segment helps in operational and strategic planning.

Customer Relationships

What type of relationship does each of our Customer Segments expect us to establish and maintain with them?
Which ones have we established?
How are they integrated with the rest of our business model?
How costly are they?

EXAMPLES
Personal Assistance
Dedicated Personal Assistance
Self-Service
Automated Services
Communities
Co-creation

* Summer reading program
* Browsing collection of popular periodicals
* Internet access through public computers
* Intralibrary loan services

Figure 6.8 Customer relationships for suburban branch library.

Care should be taken by being sensitive to cohorts whose members were discriminated against or ignored in the past. Also, most individuals are members of multiple cohorts, and so determining to which cohort to assign a cost to may be difficult. By recognizing the complexities of humans, a more empathetic and generous attitude can be taken when analyzing the costs to support services for multiple cohorts.

For the example public library, the **customer relationships** the library has created over time include a successful summer reading program for school-age children, a browsing collection of popular periodicals for its adult patrons, Internet access through dedicated public computers for unemployed adults, and intralibrary loan services for material not in the library's collection (Figure 6.8). The library's relationship with each of these patron cohorts is different depending on the specific needs of each cohort. For example, the costs of a summer reading program go beyond marketing and staff time, but the resulting positive associations children have toward the library start a relationship that hopefully will extend into adulthood.

6.2.8 Channels

The **channels** through which library patrons want to be reached have changed significantly over the past 20 years, with more services and resources being made available online for patrons to access and use from their homes or other locations that are not in the library. For most libraries' existence, the primary **channel** that patrons used was through physically entering the library. With the growth and eventual saturation of networked access through different devices and computers, library patrons are no longer

Channels

Through which Channels do our Customer Segments
want to be reached?
How are we reaching them now?
How are our Channels integrated?
Which ones work best?
Which ones are most cost-efficient?
How are we integrating them with customer routines?

* Neighborhood newsletter
* Email distribution lists
* Facebook page
* Twitter feed

Figure 6.9 Channels for suburban branch library.

required to be physically located in a library to use the library's services and collections. This new online **channel**, coupled with more services being made available online, means that libraries need to be more aware of how to serve and use these different **channels** that patrons are using to learn about the library.

Public libraries in particular have expanded their use of other sales **channels** to advertise the library's services and collections. Larger library districts use television and radio commercials to promote their services while also raising awareness among their communities of the continued relevancy of the library in those specific communities. Other channels that libraries may use include direct mailings and e-mail campaigns. For the example suburban branch library, the channels could be local neighborhood newsletters, e-mail distribution lists, a Facebook page, and a Twitter feed (Figure 6.9).

6.2.9 Revenue Streams

For a significant majority of libraries, any **revenue streams** never fully cover the total cost of operating the library. For public libraries, taxpayer support through direct taxes, bond issuance, and city taxes provides the bulk of revenue. In academic libraries, the parent institution provides most of the financial support for the library. It is in special libraries where different funding models are more prevalent, and finding different **revenue streams** follows more closely a traditional business's desire for multiple **revenue streams** to cover expenses. All libraries are interested in finding alternative **revenue streams** to supplement existing funding sources or as a way to backfill projected budget shortfalls. Libraries have already identified and implemented alternative **revenue streams** from sources such as discard book sales, copier and printing fees, overdue fines, and direct contributions to the library from donors. The incoming monies from these alternative **revenue streams** rarely are enough to make a significant contribution to the library, although these alternative **revenue streams** may make enough to make those service points that directly support those streams to be revenue and budget neutral. For example, a print service in a library may be self-supporting through print fees, but it likely does not bring significantly more revenue then the costs of supplies, equipment, and staff required for that service.

As a public or institutional good, libraries have never been seen as profit centers for most institutions or municipalities. With libraries being so dependent on external funding, changes in the financial health of the parent institution or government entity directly affect the library's operations. As libraries shift from being information providers to enablers of creative spaces, new funding opportunities arise to support these opportunities. While the library may start collecting and preserving the born-digital creations of its communities, libraries may also be able to charge for more specialized preservation services for materials being produced by their communities. Also, for those libraries whose digital properties are starting to increase in popularity, adding Web advertising may be another revenue stream that should be considered. The downside of adding advertisements is that the library has limited control over what is being sold or promoted through these online ads.

For the final example of the midsize public branch library, the library's principal revenue stream comes from a mill levy supporting their library district. The library's alternative revenue streams include a popular annual book sale, copier and printer fees, and overdue and replacement fines (Figure 6.10). These alternative revenue streams make up less than 10% of the revenue needed to cover the library's costs, although as the library looks to do some minor remodeling, a concerted effort is being made to drum up support from the local community and businesses.

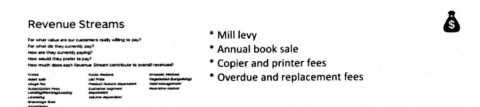

Figure 6.10 Revenue streams for a suburban branch library.

6.3 FROM BUSINESS MODEL CANVAS TO DEFINING HYPOTHESIS

The exercise of going through each of the nine categories in the business model canvas help to tease out the assumptions about a library's operations that can then be used to better define hypotheses that are critical in the build–measure–learn loop. Any new project will likely affect at least one of business model canvas's nine categories. The library can then use the business model canvas to directly associate intended outcomes of the project with important areas necessary for the library's continued operation. This should help library leadership to explain the benefits of the project to invested stakeholders of the library, such as library boards, donors, college or university administration, and interested patrons.

6.3.1 Diagramming and Visualizing Hypotheses

This chapter is mainly about constructing an explicit hypothesis from which a lean library can make predictions that can then be tested in an iterative fashion. While communicating this process to other library staff or library patrons can be difficult, a visualization method from mathematics, called category theory, can help to better communicate the assumptions and relationships of a project hypotheses in the build–measure–learn loop. Using a technique called Olog (short for ontology log), originated by David Spivak, a Massachusetts Institute of Technology mathematician, statements about realty and the relationships between those statements are described and graphically represented. Olog offers a rigorous method for knowledge representation and helps to tease out and make explicit the assumptions behind the hypotheses that may have been described and noted in one or more sections of a business model canvas for the library operation or service that is the target of a lean development or lean transformation activity occurring in the library.

This section is a brief introduction to the Olog and just skims the surface of category theory in mathematics. For those who wish for further details about Olog and category theory, Spivak's (2013) book category theory for scientists mentioned above is a good place to start. This section may use terms and descriptions of hypotheses about library services and resources that should be understood to be in a library context, and not as they may be defined in a stricter mathematical sense.

Assumptions of a project that library leadership and libraries are interested in modifying, adding, or eliminating during hypothesis generation can be described in terms of categories. The bold character **C** (for categories), is notated along with the mappings between those categories, called morphisms, which are represented as lines with arrows linking the various categories. A category, **C**, is a generic class of related objects that have morphisms—lines or mappings–between each of the objects in the category. When considering the fictitious public library branch used in the previous section about the Business Model Canvas, a simple assumption in the **key features** is diagrammed and analyzed using Olog notation. This is a way to illustrate the concepts behind a category and its morphisms and can also help to visualize the assumptions in the business model canvas.

In the Olog diagram in Figure 6.11, a **type** is a box and represents an abstract concept in the hypothesis. The label of each box is a singular indefinite noun phrase that represents not a single "book collection" but an example of a book collection. Many of these types comprise compound phrases, meaning that they are made up smaller units. **A Library Collection** is an example of a type made up of a compound phrase.

An *aspect* is a measurement, observation, or understanding of a type. In the Olog diagram in Figure 6.11, "popular books" would be regarded as a book collection. **A book collection** is **a library collection**. Each book in the **book collection** points to an existing book. "A book collection is a library collection and is a library service. An Internet connection is a library service that a library patron uses to find a book in the book collection; this object maps to a more general artifact in a library collection. A public library computer is an Internet connection, which maps to a more general service point in a library service."

Using the Olog diagram, a series of testable statements are easier to see; specific metrics can then be sought out and captured to test the

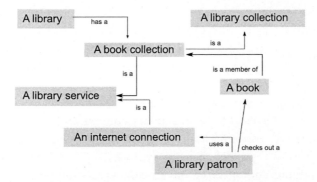

Figure 6.11 Olog diagram for a library's collection.

statement. In the Olog diagram, the following testable statements could be collected into the hypothesis, *library patrons use the Internet to find books in the library:*

- *An Internet connection is a library service* is tested with the presence of a library catalog available from the computers connected to the Internet in the library.
- *A book is a member of a book collection* is tested through querying the library's catalog.
- *A library patron checks out a book* can be tested by using circulation activity for all book resources to verify this statement.

Falsification of these statements would lead the lean library to reject the original hypothesis that *library patrons use the Internet to find books in the library*.

6.4 MANAGING COMPLEXITY THROUGH LEAN PRINCIPLES

The typical library's technological infrastructure, comprising multiple enterprise and custom applications, results in complex technology stacks. Major categories of library technology, such as an integrated library system (ILS), digital repository, and discovery layers, are usually included in a library's mixture of technology. These library-specific systems are often coupled with the broader technology of the library's Web server, e-mail, office productivity, and file servers of library staff and patrons. Together, these technologies create an ecosystem that is complex and difficult to troubleshoot. Hypothesis generation and testing can tease out and test individual components within the library's technology stack in an automated or semiautomated fashion.

An important aspect of the lean library is being able to allocate resources and money by collecting metrics. Testing the validity of hypotheses includes assessing whether these accurately reflect the situation in the library. Managers and library directors shift the library to a lean learning organization by encouraging a climate of inquiry and structured decision making. A lean library embraces the complexity of structural and technology change happening within library technology by testing its assumptions using library metrics.

Resistance to human resource allocation management based on lean startup or lean manufacturing approaches can be addressed through tools and workplace structures that engage the intellect and creativity of all employees. This empowerment of front-line employees is a hallmark of the

Toyota Production System as well as other organizations, including startups, that embrace these lean organizational principles. A company embracing lean manufacturing principles consciously and deliberately shift their quality control and processes to front-line employees on the assembly line or who directly interact with customers at any service point in the organization. Any employee is empowered to completely stop the production process based on actionable metrics generated in that step. As mentioned in an earlier chapter, the *andon* system in the Toyota Production System, where an employee can stop the assembly line when faults occur, is an example of the trust that the upper management of Toyota and other lean organizations have in the quality and judgment of their front-line workers.

While libraries are usually very responsive to reference or information queries from their patrons, libraries are not as good at finding new models and opportunities for demonstrating their value to their communities. Libraries try to fulfill patron requests for material, either by purchasing the material directly, by borrowing the material from other libraries, or by finding acceptable alternatives. For libraries to survive and even thrive in the information-rich Internet environment, a shift in librarian attitudes, perspectives, and philosophy is needed. As Godin (2011) wrote in a blog post titled "The Future of the Library," "Kids don't shlep to the library to use an out of date encyclopedia to do a report on FDR...They need a librarian more than ever (to figure out creative ways to find and use data). They need a library not at all." Later in that blog post Godin goes further and provides a wonderfully optimistic outlook for libraries that is sadly missing among many public naysayers: "There are a thousand things that could be done by a place like this [a library of creation spaces lead by knowledge and engaged librarians], all built around one mission: *take the world of data, combine it with the people in this community and create value*".

Libraries need to reformulate and streamline their operations for exploring new avenues for library services while expanding the current roles librarians have in not only initially finding information but also teaching patrons how to evaluate the veracity and validity of sources of information while applying a human context to the world of data. Meanwhile, there is more activity and creativity in public libraries that are transforming themselves from collections of physical material that is shared with their communities to centers for patrons and users to create new cultural and scholarly artifacts. This can be physically, through craft activities or three-dimensional printing, or digitally by providing technology labs for audio, video, web, and gaming creation in their communities. Academic libraries are also expanding their collection development policies to capture, collect, and manage the digital and physical assets being created by their served communities of faculty, staff, and students.

6.5 CONTINUOUS IMPROVEMENT AND INTEGRATION THROUGH STANDARDIZATION OF LIBRARY OPERATIONS

In Chapter 3, the concept of *kaizen* was introduced, along with the "five whys" technique for discovering the underlying causes of what seems to be a surface problem in a manufacturing process. When the root causes are found, the organizational and institutional knowledge for correcting the problem and errors is generalized, recorded, and communicated to the rest of the institution. Another benefit of *kaizen* that might not be apparent is that its application is also valuable in managing the complexity of library technology and operations.

Standardization of workflows and processes in lean manufacturing is a way to address the challenges of continually improving the process of producing goods and services. While the thought of standardization invokes feelings of dread and skepticism among library staff, improving the outcomes and process of library service points and collections often involves finding commonalities among different methods and then adjusting them so that the same processes can be applied to more workflows in a consistent and predictable way.

6.6 MUDA, MURI, AND MURA

6.6.1 Eliminating Waste, Avoiding Overextending, and Smoothing Variable Workflows

For many organizations, including libraries, complexity originates from a number of different sources. Processes and workflows develop over time; for libraries, this can be seen in complicated material processing, where it may take several discrete steps to order, catalog, and prep a physical book before it can be made available for circulation. Another area of increasing complexity is managing the different systems and platforms for delivering electronic resources to patrons. Often a dedicated staff member's or librarian's full-time responsibilities include managing hundreds or thousands of electronic journal subscriptions in hundreds of vendor platforms. Multiple pain points exists as library staff attempt to coordinate the management of these different resources in the library. Lean manufacturing and lean startup processes offer approaches for reducing this complexity.

In the Toyota Production System, managers and employees use three Japanese concepts, **muda**, **muri**, and **mura** to analyze a production system. **Muda**, roughly translated as **waste**, is all of the non-value-adding steps, such as moving materials to the next production station, and is the most well known of the three. **Muri** is the overburdening of people or equipment with the intent to increase productivity. This may be counterproductive if it means overextending people and resources with the end result of lower quality, low morale, and breakdowns of equipment. While libraries do not have assembly lines, **muri** can come into play when people in library systems or technical services are always in constant crisis mode—going from one emergency to another without giving library staff sufficient opportunity to catch up, reflect, or learn about the underlying causes of these ongoing problems. **Mura**, unevenness in the production schedule, is related to both **muda** and **muri**. If a production process has too much work to handle one day, and then sits idle from a lack of work the next day, that process can be described as a **mura** process. For libraries, **mura** processes may include reference sessions, book acquisitions, or other variable processes that exhibit this unevenness in patron usage or staff workloads.

Eliminating waste or looking for **muda** in library systems and technical services can help identify the "low-hanging fruit" in the physical and printed material workflows of those departments—steps in the workflow that do not directly improve the desired outcome to the process. For example, in the book processing step outlined above, the time a book waits in a cart for availability and the time spent moving a cart around to the next station are both examples of waste in the book processing workflow that are not directly contributing to moving the printed material out into the circulating collection. Removing **muda** from a such a workflow could be as simple as consolidating discrete steps into one or two steps so that the transportation **muda** for these physical items is eliminated or significantly reduced.

Overextending librarians by scheduling too many instruction sessions is an example of **muri** in a library. While these instruction sessions are a vital service, particularly in academic libraries that are trying to instruct new incoming students on basic information literacy skills, scheduling multiple sessions a day can quickly burn out the staff who are responsible for teaching them. It may not be possible to hire additional staff to teach these sessions, but there could be other mechanisms to minimize the instruction load. One such mechanism is to create short, 2- to 5-min information literacy instruction videos on frequently covered topics. Learning how to distinguish primary from secondary sources, what plagiarism is, and how to critically evaluate the creditably of online resources are all potential topics for such short instructional videos. Important but common information literacy tasks would not have to be covered in class but could be required viewing before students arrive for the instruction session. Class time could focus more on the higher-level searching and critical evaluation skills that the staff or librarian can then supplement or enhance through immediate interaction with the students.

Libraries may have little control over the variable demand for their resources and services. Libraries do have control over the best ways to schedule and respond to these demands. The application of operational changes to minimize **muda**, or this unevenness in demand, is possible.

All three of these concepts—**muri**, **muda**, and **mura**—offer ways to examine existing library systems and workflows for both explicit and hidden costs involved in the management and operation of a library.

The Tutt Library at Colorado College had a complex workflow for processing physical books from their initial purchase to the final step of adding the material to its collection. A unique aspect of the Colorado College academic year is its block plan: Students intensively study a single course's material for 3.5 weeks. In the block plan, students and, to lesser extent, faculty and staff cannot afford to wait a week if they need a book for their research or class work. To respond to students' information needs requires fast fulfillment by the library. If the library does not have a book but the work is available from a member library in the library's consortium, the Tutt Library can get the material to the student within three business days. If the book is not available from any of the member institutions in the consortium and it would take a week or more to get the material from another library, the Tutt Library typically purchases the book from Amazon.com or directly from the publisher or a book aggregator.

When a book is purchased to meet an immediate need of a student or faculty member, the book is rushed through the processing workflow of Tutt Library's technical services, skipping ahead of other material that may be in the queue in each of the steps. While the adoption of eBooks is slowly replacing the total number of books purchased by the library, this rush process is disruptive; therefore this workflow in the library was a good candidate for applying lean manufacturing concepts, particularly in an attempt to reduce complexity and improve the outcomes of this process.

6.7 CATALOG PULL PLATFORM CASE STUDY: TUTT LIBRARY BUSINESS MODEL CANVAS FOR ITS TIGER CATALOG

Creating a business modal canvas for an existing library like the Tutt Library at Colorado College is a helpful exercise. The scope of this case study is narrowed to creating a business model canvas and focuses only on the TIGER catalog project of the Catalog Pull Platform. The nine sections in the Catalog Pull Platform's business model canvas provide an overview of what the value proposition is for starting the project and its continued development.

6.7.1 Key Activities and Key Partners

The key activities for the Catalog Pull Platform are developing loosely coupled components that can be connected to provide lightweight applications for accessing and managing bibliographic and operational information about cultural heritage institutions' physical and intangible assets. Information in the Catalog Pull Platform is stored using a linked data approach, whereby triples comprising object–predicate–subject are managed and manipulated through the semantic server representation state transfer (REST) application program interface (API). The Catalog Pull Platform semantic data store uses such an open-source repository, NoSQL and search technologies like Fedora Commons, Redis, and Elasticsearch for different functionality to support catalog and digital archive applications in a distributed fashion. Each source of pull—people, institutions, and algorithms—generates requirements for functionality that can be met by combining the different components in the platform. The pull platform's analytics and metrics capture the activity each source of pull engages in with the platform, and these outcomes are tracked and reported in multiple build–measure–learn iterations for projects using the Catalog Pull Platform.

While the Catalog Pull Platform was initially developed for use by Colorado College's Tutt Library in responding to the algorithmic demands of its patrons, staff, faculty, and institutional and external parties, key partners exist both within the institution and with other organizations outside of Colorado College. The first critical partner providing consistent help and support in the development of the Catalog Pull Platform has been the Colorado College's information technology department. By providing the infrastructure to support running the Catalog Pull Platform on Linux virtual machines and by shaping the network and handling firewalls, the development and deployment of the Catalog Pull Platform was made possible with Colorado College's information technology department. Another key partner in the development of the Catalog Pull Platform is the Colorado Alliance of Research Libraries consortium. The Colorado Alliance of Research Libraries provided crucial logistical and promotional support for the Catalog Pull Platform and is an extremely important institutional pull source for generating requirements needed by its membership of institutions in the Rocky Mountain region. The final key partner is the University of Denver, which provided resources and contributed code in the development of the platform.

6.7.2 Key Resources and Cost Structures

The availability and growing maturity of a number of open-source information search and storage technologies (Fedora Commons, Elastic search, and Redis), coupled with the linked data standards work being done by schema.org, founded and supported by the major search companies, and the BIBFRAME by the Library of Congress, are all key resources for the Catalog Pull Platform and the design for the TIGER catalog. Legacy MARC records along with resource description framework representations of schema.org and BIBFRAME entities are ingested and stored in a Fedora Commons repository. These catalog entities are directly manipulated and accessed through the REST API of the semantic server operations, while Redis provides caching, analytics, and memory for the most widely used entities in the platform. This is possible only because of the collaborative and shared open-source licensing of the core technology and the growth of cloud computing infrastructure used in the broader technology markets that are controlled and developed with the support of some of the most successful startups, as well as the largest corporations.

Major costs for the Catalog Pull Platform are the human resources involved in the design, development, and support of the platform. The costs of the actual server and technology stack for the Catalog Pull Platform are quickly approaching those of any other utility and do not require hardware or software to operate and fulfill the technology needs of the library.

6.7.3 Value Propositions, Customer Segments, and Customer Relationships

As the primary and practical implementation of the Catalog Pull Platform, the TIGER catalog's main value proposition is as a replacement for the Tutt Library's expensive and commercial ILS. While currently not a feature equivalent to the legacy ILS, the TIGER catalog, even as a minimum viable product, can serve the various customer segments of Colorado College. Students, as the principal patron cohort and focus of the library, benefit from the TIGER catalog by having a consistent user experience when exploring the library's collections, no matter the source or format. The TIGER catalog offers direct ways that various cohorts can send feedback about the future design and functionality of the catalog—something that is not possible with the current library ILS. By developing and improving in an incremental fashion based on the library's usage of TIGER, the hope is that a patrons have a positive relationship as the catalog develops.

6.7.4 Channels and Revenue Streams

The primary channel that was targeted for development of the TIGER catalog is as a Web application. By using open-source and available HTML5, CSS, and Javascript libraries, the Web application is responsive and flexible enough to be used in other channels, including with mobile devices, tablets, and public kiosks.

In the early development of the TIGER catalog there was not a direct revenue stream to fund the programming of the Catalog Pull Platform. The author and principal developer of the Catalog Pull Platform has been graciously subsidized by Colorado College. Time and computing resources have been made available by the college, while other revenue streams, including consulting and programming for third parties, as well as grant opportunities, are being explored.

CHAPTER 7

Actionable Metrics from Patron Activity

7.1 ACTIONABLE METRICS FROM THE BUILD–MEASURE–LEARN CYCLE

Actionable metrics are quantitative data that directly or indirectly measure the features or characteristics of a service, resource, or system. If providing good customer service is a core value of a library, directly surveying patrons after they interact with any of the library's service points is an example of an actionable metric, assuming the survey tool accurately reflects the patrons' experiences. Examples include asking a patron leaving the library to fill out a short paper survey, or a user of the library's Web site may be prompted to take a short online survey after using the Web site, electronic database, or other online service.

In her presentation at 2012 Lean Startup Conference, Madison (2012) listed the four most important metrics for businesses to measure:

- Revenue
- Sales volume
- Customer retention
- Relevant growth

These can be reformulated as the four most important metrics for lean libraries:

- Can the library track budget sources and revenue generation in its budget?
- Can the library measure the usage of its collection? How often are these metrics being generated?
- Does the library use cohort or funnel analysis for retention of patrons, that is, engagement through both the library's online presence and its gate counts in the physical library?
- Is the size of the collection a relevant metric for growth? Are increased downloads of digital items relevant to the library? What are the statistical measurements of growth for the library? What does it mean to increase information literacy among the library's patrons?

Becoming a Lean Library
ISBN 978-1-84334-779-8

Designing effective and accurate surveys is difficult. Ambiguity in the language or framing of the feature to be captured can introduce uncertainty when trying to interpret the results later. If the questions asked confuse the respondent, then incorrect conclusions can be drawn from the data collected by the survey. The goal should be to create questions that, when answered by a library patron, result in accurate data that are able to guide the library's decisions. Based on these data, the library may choose to discontinue a service or stop paying for a little-used resource altogether. Other valid choices include continuing the service or resource, or even increasing support in relation to time and organizational energy—"doubling down" on the service or resource.

Properly framing the questions, including making the terms direct and specific enough that the questions test the hypothesis made by the library, is important. Gathering a sufficient quantity of these metrics should guide the library administration's decision making and encourage organizational learning by library staff and even patrons. Creating survey instruments and questions is beyond the scope of this chapter and book, but entire college courses and books on the topic are available for further study by the reader.

Looking beyond libraries, a general trend documented in a 2011 report from Deloitte Consulting (Hagell III, Brown, & Kulasooriya, 2011, p. 14) is that customers are becoming more "brand agnostic" when it comes to making purchasing decisions. The Internet has allowed customers to compare the features and prices of similar products, reducing the advantage large marketing campaigns have in building brand loyalty for a particular product. For libraries, this trend may partly explain the decline in relevance of the library as a primary reference source for answering questions posed by patrons and the general public.

Libraries are the custodians and stewards of a rich historical continuity of ideas from the past to the present. If libraries are to remain relevant to their parent institutions and communities, they must find and build better organizational and technical structures for responding to the networked world of almost limitless, but not free, information available online. Libraries need to adapt and evolve in this new era, responding to these changes; this may mean expanding and adopting roles and processes that are foreign to or different from what libraries traditionally specialize in. The identity of what it means to be a library may be very different from what libraries traditionally were in centuries past. With the accelerated rate of information processing and the availability of resources online, libraries should not shrink from but embrace these new challenges. This may result in the decoupling of the professional librarian from the physical repository and specific geographic location of the library.

Librarians should, however, be leery of totally separating the profession from the physical place of the library. By being the subject experts of the hyperlocal, librarians' big shift comes from also being the producers, creators, and publishers of information in their local communities.

It is not all bleak; however, even with the growth of eBooks and the expansion of devices for consuming textual material, individuals who read still prefer reading printed books by 75% (Zickur, Rainie, & Purcell, 2013). Also, as noted in the Deloitte (2011) report, there is a growing market and philosophy of sharing over purchasing, epitomized by Uber, AirBnB, Zipcar, and similar sharing services. Purchasing books and then lending them free to the library's patrons has been a defining characteristic of lending libraries over the past couple of centuries. This started with Benjamin Franklin's first lending library in Boston in the early seventeenth century and continuing to the present. Libraries should continue being known as lenders and co-creators, proud originators of a shared corpus of original scholarly and cultural works that can be adopted and extended to all sorts of industries, fields, interests, hobbies, and passions of the library's patrons.

7.2 LIBRARY PATRON ACTIVITY AS A LIBRARY ACTION METRIC

Most libraries operate in budget environments where cash inflows rarely cover the library's operational and collection expenses. Library leadership must be able to better and more quickly respond to their patrons' changing information-seeking and consumption behaviors. Much activity, thought, and effort have been expended by libraries through the various cycles of library technology development. Before the widespread adoption of integrated library systems (ILSs) in libraries, generating circulation statistics of a library's physical collection was labor intensive and sporadic. Most modern commercial and open-source ILSs track basic metrics on what material circulates among a library's patrons. Activities being tracked usually include the total number of checkouts, the last time material was checked out, if material is currently checked out, and when items are due back to the library.

Other sources for library patron activity include resource-sharing requests and fulfillment of library materials, in-library and online reference sessions, and tracking of Web site and online resources usage. Resource sharing, whether through a library consortium or through direct library-to-library lending, is usually managed through a service or product that may provide immediate access to usage statistics. Tracking statistics from library reference services runs across the spectrum. From tick marks made on paper, to custom client-side databases made with Microsoft Access software, to full products purchased from vendors, the quality and depth of information from reference services at a library can vary considerably. Tracking patron activity online can be as simple as a Web server log analysis to the very sophisticated capabilities of Google Analytics or other commercial analytics software. From these metrics, the library can start to create profiles of library patrons using the library.

While patron activity is traditionally tied to usage metrics of particular collections in the library, other activities of the library should also be included. Instruction activities, such as bibliographic and information literacy training, are often tracked by collecting simple demographic information as well as the student's attendance in the instruction session. Patron instruction and education is another area of library activity that is used by library leadership to demonstrate the value of the library to external parties and stakeholders. Instruction sessions also lend themselves well to tracking specific outcomes by the library's patrons. Using before-and-after testing, specific information literacy goals or objectives can be tracked and collected. By being direct and explicit about what the library is trying to accomplish through the educational session, it can then be constructed in a lean fashion using a build–measure–learn iterative process.

7.3 THE MYTH OF THE MONOLITHIC LIBRARY PATRON

A common business fallacy is the assumption that its customers are all alike, sharing similar demographics, ideas, and attitudes, with the business lumping all of these customers into categories that are too broad. Libraries often overgeneralize the activity and characteristics of their patrons by categorizing them into a few groups, such as children and adults. A young child just beginning to read has very different reading and information instruction needs than a middle-school adolescent wanting to check out the latest popular young adult novel. Similarly, a retiree seeking the latest best seller has different expectations than a middle-aged unemployed adult searching for career advice and information.

Depending on the type of library, how patrons are divided into groups—called "cohorts" in lean startup terminology—is an important exercise when analyzing patrons. A library's process of categorizing patrons into cohorts should be revisited periodically as the library responds to changes in its environment. For a public library, patron cohorts such as adults, seniors, and children are common, whereas for an academic library, typical cohorts include faculty, students, and the public. Cohorts are sometimes identified through tracking activity, with those categories then being used for evaluation and comparison purposes.

Dividing a library's patrons into different and identifiable groups is useful for library leadership to gauge how well services and collection development decisions are meeting the needs of the library's communities. The library's services and resources have different impacts depending on the specific needs of each cohort. Instead of overly broad generalizations, like asserting that all patrons now want to be able to borrow eBooks, cohort analysis teases out the differences in service demands among the library's various patrons. Part of the process to capture the library's cohorts' different impressions and use of library services extends as well to the library's electronic services and resources. A primary school student's search behavior differs from that of an adult community college student when using the library's online catalog or discovery service.

Breaking patrons into cohorts when analyzing electronic resource usage may be difficult. For example, if the library's catalog is accessible from public kiosks that do not require patrons to log in or identify themselves, then it is almost impossible to analyze cohorts based on demographic data collected from these kiosks, although efforts have been made to compensate by using short online surveys. Similarly, remote access to the library's discovery services may not provide the necessary granularity that lends itself to cohort analysis of the library's patrons. The danger of drawing inaccurate conclusions increases without the ability to identify cohorts. The library starts overgeneralizing usage trends and believes that their patrons all have similar needs and information requirements.

7.4 THE LONG TAIL OF LIBRARY COHORTS

Libraries need to operate and excel in providing selection, curation, and discoverablity of resources and services that appeal to ever more narrowly defined cohorts. The expansion of the Internet has brought out and sharply defines the specific and important differences that exist in varying degrees among all library users.

Finding the right balance between broad versus narrow cohorts is important. A danger of becoming too specific when defining and tracking different cohorts is that the increased costs in collecting and evaluating the data overwhelm the benefits that such distinctions of patrons in the data may bring to the library. The information overhead of tracking and managing the different data streams can be too much; it may be necessary to consolidate different library patron cohorts if those specific cohorts exhibit and generate similar activity metrics. The lack of functionality and differences between, for example, second- and third-year undergraduates at a four-year college or university, which can affect the ability to make decisions, may mean consolidating both into a single cohort, thereby reducing the time needed to generate, collect, and respond to activity metrics. The balancing act to determine the optimal number of cohorts occurs between generating actionable metrics and being too specific in cohort identification that the analysis of the metrics is blurred and confounded.

The ultimate goal of the Toyota Production System is to reduce the batch size of production to a single unit. Applying this idea to libraries means that, instead of trying to group patrons into cohorts, library resources and services would be targeted to the specific individual. Again, however, librarians need to balance their duty to patrons by preserving their privacy and autonomy without becoming too intrusive. The goal should always be transparency, and libraries should always opt-in for more tracking in the library and delivering customized services to the library's patrons. This is even more important as library systems become more complex and library staff depend on the services of for-profit companies or nonprofits that act as for-profit companies.

7.5 GOOGLE ANALYTICS

Many libraries use a service from Google, called Google Analytics, to track and report the user activity on their public Web sites and other Web properties such as digital repositories. While concerns exist about patron privacy with the use of Google Analytics, using Google Analytics in targeted and specific ways can minimize the collection of identifiable patron activity or the association of individual patrons with their behavior. If a library vendor's product uses Google Analytics, but the vendor is not forthcoming about their own data mining efforts, concerns should be raised by library leadership. Striking the right balance between the privacy of the individual over their demand for customization and personalization is not just a library challenge—it is faced by many other organizations and corporations.

When considering a product or service, a library must assume that patrons' data are being monitored and mined by both governments and corporations.

As Edward Snowden's revelations of the extensive capturing of users' activities by the National Security Agency exposed the United States governmental efforts toward capturing massive amounts of user data by colluding with the largest corporate software and telecommunication companies to surreptitiously monitor their users were ongoing. Another danger is a library's data being fed to the large and shadowy world of corporate monitoring and criminal scams, spam e-mails, and other fraudulent activities online.

Given all these caveats, Google Analytics is very useful as a tool to track characteristics of users, although it does not directly associate with specific patrons by library. Just by using Google Analytics, individual online activity is being captured and associated with specific patrons.

Google Analytics breaks down Web users and, now by necessity, mobile users by the following characteristics:

1. Source of Web traffic, including Internet service provider and geographic locations
2. Operating system and Web browser version
3. Mobile and desktop
4. Alerts for changes in metrics or collection of metrics (called "segments" in Google Analytics)
5. Real-time Web traffic broken down by location, traffic source, content events, and conversions
6. Web site audience organized by demographics, patron interests, and geographic location
7. Behaviors such as a new versus returning user, frequency, and most recent visit.

These characteristics become even more useful if the library is gauging the impacts of the design and functionality of a new or existing product or service. Google Analytics also offers ways to embed custom variables to track specific metrics that can be included in the source code of the library's ILS or Web site. Later in this chapter, we examine how to use Google Analytics to test two slightly different Web design variants, called A/B testing or cohort testing, to see which version affects such metrics as increasing the usage of a library service or decreasing the number of visitors who never use any of the library's services. In a lean library system, identified cohorts could be set to a variable denoting a specific type; for example, if the library patron cohort is a public patron, that sets a usage variable to be reported through Google Analytics.

Google Analytics also offers visualizations of patron activity that are helpful to spot trends and areas of concern. The decline in the usage of an expensive digital resource is easier to explain and understand if it is depicted in a graph. These visualizations can do a better job of summarizing and answering the questions initially asked by the hypothesis after being tested by the actionable metrics collected and analyzed by Google Analytics.

7.6 COUNTER DATABASE STATISTICS

For academic, public, special, and K-12 libraries, electronic journal databases are often the largest expense—or second-largest expense after labor costs—of the library. To justify this large expenditure of resources, most vendors provide usage statistics in the COUNTER (Counting Online Usage of Networked Electronic Resources) format. COUNTER is an international effort targeting a standard format and the content of patron usage of these large databases.

Implementing COUNTER allows a common vocabulary and data for cross-product comparisons that can assist libraries, publishers, and associated support companies. At the Tutt Library, librarians and the director of the library have approximately monthly collection development committee meetings to allocate the library's collection budget. Decisions regarding allocation often hinge on actionable metrics, particularly cost per usage, as a gross evaluation of how much these resources are being used by the library's patrons.

When making collection development decisions, first ask what information, if available, would be convincing enough to add a new resource? Or, conversely, what information would be convincing enough to stop subscribing to a resource? The gross statistic provided in a vendor's COUNTER statistics provides only a raw number for such things as click count, unique visitors, and PDF or page downloads. Trying to normalize these statistics across a broad portfolio of resources can be difficult because different vendors interpret the requirements for COUNTER statistical results in different ways. The vendors may not be explicit or forthcoming to librarians about the underlying assumptions they are using in capturing or calculating these numbers. Other institutions have different mechanisms, including collection quotas, governmental grants, and other formulas, to allocate funds for electronic resources.

Other issues with ambiguity and lack of transparency create incentives for vendors to attempt to manipulate or simply not provide COUNTER statistics for their products (Welker, 2012). While COUNTER statistics are very important for the evaluation process, they address only one of two ways collection decisions are made by libraries. An important second component of these decisions is how specific cohorts of patrons use the materials. For example, a specialized subject database may have a high cost-per-usage ratio compared with a more general topic source but offers essential material for use by specific patron cohorts served by the library. This important secondary analysis often lacks any method for tracking specific patron cohorts, but having this information would be important to the library.

7.7 PASSIVE VERSUS ACTIVE METRICS

Libraries must also consider ways they can directly improve their processes through more active management of patron activity and library workflows. How might direct collection of patron activity be justified and promoted in a way that aligns with the library's values of patron privacy while also giving the patron the maximum amount of information on the extent and depth of metric gathering in the library? Two ways to accomplish this are, first, to be transparent from the beginning about the library's policies toward gathering, collecting, and storing metrics about patron activity. The second is giving library patrons the opportunity and ability to opt-in to any communication activity on channels like e-mail, SMS/text, Facebook messaging, mobile applications, or any new communication modality that may be developed in the future. While the challenges of correctly assessing the library system or service become more complicated with extensive privacy controls available to patrons, this means the library may have to rely more on passive metrics that may not require the patron's consent because the data have been sufficiently anonymized.

Technology companies have a horrible record when it comes to collecting metrics on their users. As Hailbel (2014) convincingly iterated, technology firms have an economic incentive to use user interface ploys to trick users in engaging with advertisements, to sign up for unwanted e-mail newsletters, or to have their personal contacts raided and their friends and family spammed by these often shadowy corporations.

Here, a simple distinction is made between passive and active metrics. Active metrics are metrics that require the patron's consent. This consent becomes immediately hazy when the library relies on third-party reporting structures, such as Google Analytics, that definitely collect the direct activity of the patron without providing him or her with the ability to refuse participation in the data-collecting activity. Online tracking often involves many intermediaries that have no obligation to inform the patron of the data collected nor give the patron the opportunity to opt out of the data collected about their online activities.

7.8 A/B TESTING AS AN ACTIVE METRIC

Cohort testing, better known as A/B testing, is a foundational method of creating and generating actionable metrics in lean startup methodology. In A/B testing, two or more user interface options, such as use of the terms *stacks* versus *shelves* to describe the location of a physical book in the library, are randomly presented to a patron accessing the Web service. The A/B test usually lasts for a specific length of time, and the Web traffic between the options is compared to see which version performs better, usually by look-ing at differences in the click counts between the options. In the library example above, the term clicked on most by patrons helps the design of the Web service by decreasing patron confusion and improving positive out-comes. In the classic version of A/B testing, all Web traffic is evenly divided between two versions of a Web page, and the results are then compared and action taken based on those metrics.

While A/B testing of user interface elements of library Web sites can offer important insights into the library's patrons, A/B testing does have problems for consideration by library leadership. Like any statistical test, A/B testing requires a minimum number of users to generate statistically significant results to determine whether the library's community prefers one option over another. This can be difficult, particularly for smaller libraries that may not be able to generate enough interest or traffic volume among its patrons to achieve a confidence level that is commonly accepted for actionable and accurate differences. Even worse, a statistically small sample size could skew the interpretation, resulting in an erroneous conclusion that one option should be preferred over another when that decision is not supported by the evidence.

Another problem with A/B testing is when the options being tested are not distinct enough or different enough from each other. In the initial exam-ple of a library testing *stacks* versus *shelves*, the two terms by themselves might not be different enough to generate an actionable result. If the differences are not distinct enough, the resulting data—even for a large sample size—may show similar results for both options. Inconclusive results can be frustrating, especially when the library project may be on a tight deadline or if the options seem different enough to the library staff involved in the design.

This chapter's case study is about the second iteration of Colorado College's TIGER catalog using the semantic server and other components of the Catalog Pull Platform. The author and main developer wanted to see whether patrons preferred an initial display with a facet list expanded, as is the default for most library discovery layers, or a display with the facet list hidden and part of a different layer filter option.

Google Analytics provides a number of tools that can assist a library when doing its own A/B testing to choose which design element to use in a new user interface. Google Analytics offers a variant of A/B testing called *"multiarmed bandit"* testing, where multiple options can be tested at the same time. Using Google Analytics along with some of its features is explored in the next section.

7.9 CATALOG PULL PLATFORM CASE STUDY: A/B TESTING AND PRIVACY

The Catalog Pull Platforms try to maintain a balance between generating meaningful actionable metrics from patrons while still respecting patrons' privacy in the context of libraries' strong defense of that privacy. It is in the tension between these two counterforces that the predictive promise of personalization versus individual privacy can make a striking balance in engineering choices between the two difficult, but not impossible. In the Catalog Pull Platform, any information on patron activity that is automatically collected is done so to minimize any personally identifiable data. For most of the user interface and functionality testing, Internet protocol (IP) addresses are stored instead of any user accounts or other patron-identifiable data. While this design and implementation can make it difficult to provide a totally customizable search and user interface that is as responsive to a patron's information needs as commercial search engines, the Catalog Pull Platform does allow for the collection of patron-specific and identifiable information only when specifically and explicitly opted into by the patron. Patrons, librarians, and staff user accounts in the Catalog Pull Platform allow for search history to be collected and managed by the individual while providing a mechanism for managing the collection through staff privileges.

In the third build–measure–learn iteration of the Catalog Pull Platform, individuals visiting the catalog were presented with a choice of how to filter the results that are returned from the search index. The first option presented a fully expanded tree widget with three different ways to reduce the result set: by location in the library; by the format, type, or carrier medium of the item; and, finally, by the publication date. The second option did not display the facet widget but did include an indicator next to the displayed total number of items, which, if clicked, displayed the expanded facet tree widget.

When doing A/B testing, the hypothesis that the Tutt Library wanted to test was whether displaying the search widget on the first page of results in the Catalog Pull Platform increased the usage of the facet's filtering versus keeping the display of the search results almost identical to the first design. Any patron-identifiable information was not captured or collected, only the patron's computer or mobile device IP address.

The options for this A/B test were

- *Option A*: Do not show a facet widget upon the initial display of the catalog search results (the null hypothesis for this test).
- *Option B*: Show an expanded facet widget upon the initial display of the catalog search results (the alternative hypothesis for this test).

An actionable metric for this A/B test was captured and collected, that is, tracking the increase in click count for the null hypothesis (option A) versus the alternative hypothesis (option B). A confounding factor in this A/B test was the addition of a slight visual cue displaying the facet widget in the user interface design for the null hypothesis. Ideally, this slight visual cue (a clickable arrow next the total number of items in this result set) would have had its own A/B testing with the original design, but, like most engineering projects, sacrifices and compromises were needed to continue progress on the project.

A major problem with A/B testing is not having enough tests to be statistically significant. With the minimum number of impressions being approximately 6000, this level of engagement for such a catalog as that at Colorado College'Tutt Library would need to run significantly longer than the approximately 1 month per iteration in this build–measure–learn iteration of the Catalog Pull Platform.

CHAPTER 8

Pivoting or Persevering when Technology Changes

During the development, marketing, and selling of a new product or server, lean startups and other entrepreneurial enterprises may arrive at critical junctions that require informed decisions on whether the organization should continue along its current development path or change its product or service focus. This process of deciding and implementing this change is called a *pivot* in lean startup terminology. The risks of starting development in another product or service may be difficult to justify if growth is not meeting the expectations of the startup's founders and investors. These decision points are arrived at for multiple reasons: the market changes, sales and usage of the product are failing to meet the startup's expectations, or the startup sees a new opportunity. The decision to pivot often comes from a combination of these factors. This chapter uses the framework of the lean startup to provide guidance for the library manager in deciding to continue on an existing technology path or to pivot to a new service or technology based on a considered and metric-based approach.

The decision to continue, to persevere, or to pivot in a different direction occurred to the author in the development trajectory of his open-source library services platform. In the early 2010s, Jeremy Nelson's work on the Redis Library Services Platform was showing promise and receiving national recognition by the Library of Congress. The Redis Library Services Platform focused on providing Django (a Web platform) applications that interfaced with a commercial integrated library system (ILS), a digital repository using Fedora, and key-value bibliographic data storage using Redis.

While Colorado College was the only institution to actively use the Redis Library Services Platform, the University of Wyoming attempted to run the platform to perform one action using the Fedora Utilities app that was successfully deployed and widely used by staff at Colorado College. The Redis Library Services Platform was developed and deployed using virtual machines running Ubuntu Linux, whereas the University of Wyoming staff required the platform to run on their Microsoft Windows workstations. Nelson was able to run the Redis Library Services Platform on his Microsoft Windows workstation, but the process was complex and convoluted and was difficult to get running within his collaborators' environment in Wyoming.

Becoming a Lean Library
ISBN 978-1-84334-779-8

In the Redis Library Services Platform, the richness and usability of Django came with a price: The apps were too tightly coupled with each other and with Django. Many of the core software libraries used on the Redis Library Services Platform either did not exist on Microsoft Windows or required running questionable Windows executables along with editing environmental settings on the computer. Become of the tight coupling of app functionalities with each other, running isolated apps without a few critical components was impossible.

The inability to expand the usage of the Redis Library Services Platform beyond one institution, the tight coupling of functionality between the apps, and more development effort being devoted to improving the functionality and usability of the app interface to the Colorado College's Fedora digital repository were all reasons that suggested to Nelson that a pivot might be in order, despite the success of the current development path. In the autumn of 2013, Nelson started a collaboration with Aaron Schmidt's (2013) simplified online catalog for use by library patrons. While the initial prototype was developed using the Redis Library Services Platform, this simplification refocused Nelson on the larger ideas behind his design of and the implementation decisions made on the Redis Library Services Platform. After successfully using another Python-based Web microframework called Flask for various online presentations, Nelson realized that evidence and analytics supporting a pivot were available. Instead of focusing on multiple apps running in a Django environment—some with no connection to Redis—Nelson decided to pivot and start work on a much looser platform he later called the Catalog Pull Platform, first mentioned in the Introduction to this book. This pivot illustrates many of the lessons that are analyzed in this chapter.

Leaders, regardless of their position in an organization, should guard against being too emotionally attached to any current or existing technology. One of the most difficult aspects of making a pivot is the ego and investment already sunk into the current line of business. This can be especially difficult when the existing idea, product, or service is still viable, deserves attention, and has intrinsic value. Here are three considerations when considering a pivot in library technology:

- Does the technology require extensive staff training to use effectively?
- Does the technology require much back-and-forth communication between the vendor and library to resolve what seem like simple problems?
- Is the technology's value position questionable, with the total cost of ownership of the product or service difficult to estimate and the costs the library too high?

Based on the answers to these questions, library leadership should start looking for alternatives—alternatives that share more of the characteristics of a pull platform. A pull platform includes not only the technology itself but also the people and work processes that together combine into a responsive and cohesive service that pulls together a diverse set of inputs; these inputs can be extremely variable but produce standard outputs and data feeds for inclusion in other stages or aspects of the platform, including third-party nonprofits, other libraries, and commercial vendors.

If the library's technology is shifted to a pull platform, making pivots when the environment shifts as a result of external factors, such as budget cuts or decreased demand from the patrons for traditional library services, should be easier. Internal factors such as key personnel leaving the library could also be opportunities for a technology pivot as well. A significant problem for library technology is that the choices, especially for library-specific technology, may be limited to one or two roughly equivalent alternatives. In this situation, switching costs may not justify dropping the current product or service for an alternative that is roughly equivalent. When there are limited choices between similar products, the next best thing is to look for ways the current technology can be extended and built upon to better meet the library's requirements. Like the startup founders trying to decide to continue with an existing product or shift to a new area of business, library leadership can use these techniques to evaluate critically the existing product or service and better prepare the library to switch to a new product or service if one becomes available.

8.1 PIVOTING

Libraries, while not as flexible as entrepreneurial startups, can still change direction when significant technology disruption occurs. Libraries that modify operations and invest in new technology with compassion and care toward the current staff can help the entire library respond in a flexible manner. In lean startups, pivoting is driven by metrics that predict whether continuing on the current development path will not achieve the desired outcomes, even if maintaining the status quo is currently profitable for the startup.

Similarly, a library may not feel any urgency to invest in a new technology or to change significantly its operations to accommodate new demands by its patrons. The signals the library uses, such as circulation statistics or gate counts, could be holding steady or slightly improving. What these comforting metrics can mask is that usage of the library by patrons may be declining in absolute terms as they seek alternative methods and companies provide similar information better, with more convenience to the library's existing patrons.

To continue being a viable and engaged member in the communities it serves, a library must continually seek out and respond to new challenges, recasting them as opportunities. Libraries are just part of entire industries that need to modify and change their current operations as an uncertain future approaches. Similar to the process in lean startups, pivoting a library product or service should be a metric-driven decision process. In both cases, changing or pivoting should happen if the data support such a decision—not because of personal involvement or entanglements.

As libraries respond to changing demands from patrons, such as requests for easier-to-use eBook platforms, they need to determine what services and resource allocations will meet these changing demands. Maintaining the library's core services and resources depends on the demand by library patrons and by the judgment of the library leadership. These small pivots usually does not rise to the level of a complete pivoted experienced by a startup discontinuing a current service or product line in favor of developing a significant departure from its current business. Libraries can use lean startup methodology to determine whether a pivot should occur in an existing library resource or service.

Retraining and reallocating staff involve costs that should be included in any decision to pivot. Failing to do so because of fear and concern about the impact on staff should be minimized by being transparent as possible during the decision-making process. Using a lean approach that fully embraces the measurement of and knowledge from workflows that use technology to meet patron demands, coupled with staff education about lean processes, help to shift staff attitudes toward the changes brought on by the pivot from being reactive and reactionary to one that embraces the opportunity to explore new ways and technology to meet the challenges facing the library.

8.2 PERSEVERANCE

Libraries' response to technology change differs from that of a lean startup. A number of factors beyond the library's control, including poor economic conditions or reduced higher-education funding, limit libraries' ability to pivot. Libraries often have had decades to build and implement workflows using legacy software and services. It would be too expensive and disruptive in the short term for libraries' operations and services to move away from these legacy software systems to newer software. Perhaps library patrons and staff are so accustomed to the current status quo that the library administration's reflex is to continue or persevere in the current environment while ignoring or discounting the demands for newer technology.

Examples of libraries that rely on antiquated hardware abound, such as using dot-matrix printers for printing book labels because the library's ILS does not, or cannot, support even commodity label printers. Other situations include intralibrary loan software that needs to run a depreciated operating system on old hardware because the software cannot run under the latest version of the Windows operating system. Ideally, lean library technology should be flexible enough to implement or replace such legacy systems as needed, instead of requiring a large investment in an entirely new and expensive ILS. Over time, as the Catalog Pull Platform matures, it will someday be possible to fully replace a legacy ILS with a technically superior product that is simple enough to run for a small library system with part-time staff and scalable for entire regional and national collections.

This conservatism hinders library leadership from making needed changes in its operations and technology. New demands may ultimately result in patrons forgoing the library in favor of commercial products and services. This may not affect the higher end of the economic spectrum, but it does create distinct barriers to using these new online and electronic services among the economically disadvantaged. Libraries need better methods and processes for identifying when to pivot away from current technology toward newer services and technology. Cloud-based technologies are starting to make inroads in libraries by freeing them from hosting and managing the complete technology stack.

Most libraries do not have the skills or infrastructure to develop totally customized solutions for library services. However, a library may need to radically reorganize its systems and technical services such that existing and new products and services are better integrated with each other. Libraries work must provide a user experience that differs from what a patron would get from any of the alternatives. This is often difficult when legacy platforms or software does not provide access points, often called application program interfaces, keeping a library from integrating the technology into their own public services.

For many years, libraries faced little competition as information providers and curators. This not the case in our current age of Google, Twitter, Facebook, Instagram, or Quora. Direct online collaboration through audio and video conferencing, e-mail listservs, mobile apps, or newsletters offer alternative information sources distinct from a library. Especially, salespeople hawking the latest discovery product deny or downplay the reality that patrons most likely did not start their search from the library's discovery layer or catalog. What the library may need to start doing instead is to ensure their collections are easily linkable and associated with the library, exposing this information for harvesting by Web search crawlers or allowing it to be embedded easily into the Twitter, LinkedIn, and Facebook streams of their patrons and staff.

8.3 AGILE DECISION POINT

When a lean library decides that a change is needed, the next decision is how the library will change a service or resource. If the metrics being generated by the current process are not encouraging, the decision to shift to a different service or technology, or to reallocate personnel, must be made. At this tipping point, a library can respond in an agile fashion to minimize the disruption to the library's staff and patrons.

If the evidence is not supportive of an existing service, a library leader should convincingly argue that change is needed to both their supervisors, board of directors, and staff. In an ongoing build–measure–learn loop, experience guides the leader's intuition, backed by supportive statistics, that a decision point has been reached. When conflicting evidence exists or there is increasing uncertainty in the foundational assumptions, the experienced leader recognizes this and responds accordingly. A characteristic of a good hypothesis is that these foundational assumptions are falsifiable, or can be proved wrong with the available evidence.

Risks, such as vendor lock-in, lack of programmable access points, and difficulty supporting the system, are associated with continuing financial and organizational support for legacy systems. A newer system or service can be changed and implemented if an external decision maker is interested in a new technology. While catering to specific individuals tastes is not recommended, impassioned or engaged advocates should be cultivated by library leadership. These advocates are useful for getting support from more reluctant members of the library's staff and community when considering a pivot in a library-provided technology or service. The communities that seek out the critics or the nonusers of the library and try engage their skepticism toward the library's efforts can offer new directions or possibilities. Consider the criticism as an opportunity to identify areas that the library can pivot or start supporting.

Libraries need to shift their standard cataloging practices and operations from individually customizing and processing bibliographic records for popular or common material, even if it is merely downloading a machine-readable catalog (MARC) record from the Online Computer Library Center and adding a holdings statement and local call number. This type of duplicating copy-cataloging should decrease with more efforts by the library during original cataloging. With the new roles of libraries becoming publishers and curators of locally produced cultural and scholarly materials created by their communities, original cataloging becomes even more important. For academic libraries, collecting and ingesting students, faculty, and staff's creative output into institutional repositories is just a first step in being a locally creditable steward and promoter of this material.

For public libraries, curating and developing programming and resources for popular subjects of interest to their communities is another way libraries should pivot in their resources and efforts and differentiate themselves from other information providers. Providing makerspaces and creation spaces, lending nontraditional tools and providing three-dimensional printing opportunities, and being creative curators and publishers are all ways public libraries are pivoting to new roles for their communities.

8.4 DISRUPTION OCCURS

The focus of this chapter has been on helping libraries decide when to continue a service or resource, or to make sometimes radical changes to resource allocation or a service. Change based on technology is certainly not new for libraries. Audio and video format changes have required libraries to stop purchasing audio formats like LP and cassettes and start collecting compact discs, and change from VHS video cassettes to DVDs and Blu-ray discs. In the past, libraries have had to adapt their materials budget, weeding out older formats in favor of new, although many libraries still maintain collections of these older formats because the material is not available in the new format or because of support and demand for these formats by a subset of their patrons. Certainly, this habit of libraries can be advantageous; older formats may offer new explorations by younger patrons, for example, in the small, but growing, preference for vinyl LPs of music by Millenials.

Is there a magic tipping point—a set or mixture of metrics and analytics that instantly and reliably inform collection management or the library administration to continue funding an existing technology or shift to a newer one? In the past, these decisions were often driven by hunches of library personnel or by patrons' requests for new technology. So, are there ranges for recommendations? Are there better ways to position the library to keep serving their current uses while still being able to respond to requests for new technology?

8.5 RESPONDING THROUGH TENKAN

In the modern martial art of Aikido, a fundamental movement called *tenkan* is taught, starting with beginning students and continued practice by high-ranking instructors. In tenkan, an individual starts with one foot forward and then turns—or pivots—180° around the forward foot so that he or she is now facing in the opposite direction. In this manner, a frontal attack by an opponent can be avoided with tenkan by the responding individual while putting him or her into a safer location and in a better strategic position to respond.

Using tenkan as a metaphor, organizations like libraries sometimes need to make radical shifts in their perspectives, operations, and strategic planning to respond effectively to disruptive forces. Much like the raison d'être for a martial art (staying alive even when confronted with superior strength), agile organizations are able to respond to complex circumstances through the use of tools and processes such as the build–measure–learn loop (Chapter 4), the business model canvas and hypothesis generation (Chapter 6), to finally various sources of actionable metrics (Chapter 7).

The focus of the next chapter, *DevOps as a Lean Strategy* brings together the creative impulses of a library's communities with the simple requirement that operational technology in the library work.

8.6 CATALOG PULL PLATFORM CASE STUDY: PIVOTING WITH TECHNOLOGY CHANGE

There have been a number of pivots during the implementation history of the Catalog Pull Platform. This case study examines the initial large pivot by the Tutt Library when switching from Django in the Redis Library Services Platform to the Catalog Pull Platform using Flask and Node.js.

8.6.1 Background

The technology pivots in the development of the Catalog Pull Platform started with the programming expertise and experience of the platform's primary developer, Jeremy Nelson. As an undergraduate at Knox College (a private liberal arts college in Illinois) in the early 1990s, Nelson became fascinated with the early Internet, staring with using Gopher on one of two public, Internet-connected computers at Knox College's library. As a junior he was introduced to the first Web browser, Mosaic from the National Center for the Supercomputing Applications, and browsed the early Web while starting to build websites in HTML.

Nelson's entire career in technology has been about pivoting and exploring emerging technologies and adopting these new ideas and technologies to solve organizations' current problems. Before becoming a librarian, Nelson worked in a variety of technology positions in a number of different software and financial services companies. He started in project management and support roles and later became a programmer and systems designer. Nelson has used a variety of programming languages and frameworks over the course of his career, including Delphi, TUTOR, Java, Javascript, and Python. He also worked on back-end data representations and data storage, starting with a propitiatory BTree database, Oracle, XML, XSLT, and JSON, and later with NoSQL technologies like Redis and MongoDB.

8.6.2 Aristotle Discovery Layer and Redis Library Services Platform

When Nelson started working as the metadata and systems librarian at Colorado College in 2010, he began investigating two open-source discovery layer library projects: VuFind and Blacklight. VuFind, a PHP-based project, and Blacklight, a Ruby-on-Rails project, both provided Web front ends to a Solr search index. Of the two, Blacklight seemed the easiest to experiment with, and a demo instance of Blacklight was implemented using the more than 800,000 MARC records exported from Tutt Library's commercial ILS. Blacklight provided inspiration with the key insight that a modern Web development framework could support sophisticated discovery layers, but Nelson was more comfortable developing in Python. He had already started creating productivity scripts for the library's manipulation database vendor-provided MARC records in Python. Because the Tutt Library's systems and cataloging departments were very lean, Nelson was the primary developer for the library, with help from his systems staff of one and other librarians.

Not wanting to maintain different code bases in multiple programming languages, and realizing that using either VuFind or Blacklight would require extensive customization for Colorado College, Nelson decided to fork a branch from a dormant Django-based discovery layer called Kochief, which became the basis for the new project, the Aristotle Discovery Layer (http://discovery.coloradocollege.edu/).

In 2011 Nelson started researching Redis, an open-source NoSQL key-value data store, as a way to represent bibliographic entities, first with transforming MARC21 to functional requirements for bibliographic records entities and later with the introduction of the Library of Congress's BIBFRAME environment. This experimentation of converting Tutt Library's MARC records into BIBFRAME, and later the schema.org metadata vocabularies, continued to progress with a number of presentations at regional and national library conferences, including the American Library Association's 2013 annual conference in Chicago, Illinois. As 2013 went on, some limitations of Redis become more noticeable, including the biggest problem of running out of memory when trying to ingest all MARC records into Redis. Even when Colorado College's information technology department doubled the server memory of the virtual machine running the instance, it insufficient for ingesting all of the MARC records.

8.6.3 Fedora 4, Flask, and Node.js in the Catalog Pull Platform

Pivoting from projects that focused on the middleware and data store did not fully describe or capture all of the different types of small Web applications, among which the only thing in common was the same Django middleware and front-end HTML5 app design. Instead of making the focus of the work the implementation technology (in the case of the Redis Library Services Platform), a pivot was made to move to a better description of what Nelson and the Tutt Library were trying to do, namely, create a platform that accurately described and summarized the intentions of the technology suite being developed at Colorado College.

Fedora 4 is the latest release of the open-source digital repository under the guidance of the DuraSpace Organization. With its design as an intentional linked data platform with a representation state transfer create–update–read–delete for digital objects, the platform allows Web addresses and resources to be created with associated linked-data resource description framework graphs associated with those new objects. This was the major feature for the Catalog Pull Platform because it fulfilled two key requirements: a way to preserve and manage the legacy MARC records while natively supporting the new linked-data vocabularies such as BIBFRAME, RDA Registry, and schema.org.

Redis was still a critical component of the platform as an analytic and cache for the main applications. Together, MongoDB and Redis are the core technology in the Catalog Pull Platform's semantic server.

The smaller secondary pivot that coincided with the adoption of Fedora 4 for the primary data storage was the shift from using Django to Flask as the Web framework. Flask (a Python micro–Web framework) design and implementation followed a looser coupled model that fit better than the comprehensive but tightly coupled model of Django. The switch to Flask from Django used in the Discovery Layer made the development of Tutt Library's new catalog (http://catalog.coloradocollege.edu/), with the design inspired by Aaron Schmidt's design work for a public catalog.

Finally, to support a new minimum viable product of a consortium union catalog using the Catalog Pull Platform, Node.js was suggested as an alternative to Python Web frameworks. Node.js, a Javascript Web back end, was investigated as the middleware because of its support for large, scaleable Web applications.

Throughout the development history of the Catalog Pull Platform, pivoting with technology change is an important characteristic that supported the shift of Tutt Library's technology to a lean model, starting with the Aristotle Discovery Layer, moving to the Redis Library Services Platform, and finally settling on a more platform-based approach to supporting pull sources of the library in the Catalog Pull Platform.

CHAPTER 9

DevOps as a Lean Strategy

DevOps, an amalgamation of the words *development* and *operations*, is different from the traditional approach information technology (IT) departments in enterprises program a new product or service. In software development the term *waterfall development* refers to a development process that starts with a detailed and extensive project plan that breaks down the proposed project into a separate and discrete steps. The first step is gathering requirements from interviews and research with the end users of the software product, followed by a technical design and user interface design step. This leads to the programming step and then a quality assurance step, ending with the final release and support of the software project. Each step must be substantially completed before the next step starts project planning and execution. One of the biggest problems with the waterfall method is that requirements change and shift during long project periods, and if those changes are significant, costly delays can result. Another significant problem with waterfall development is that end users of the software may participate only in the requirements gathering phase, with limited participation in the user interface and quality assurance phases through to when the final developed product is released. This makes it more difficult to change the software if it is missing functionality needed by the end user.

Even the most rigid and bureaucratic of libraries, with strict separations of job responsibilities, divisions, and employees, should consider adopting DevOps for their IT departments. DevOps is becoming a more popular trend in corporations of all sizes, including Fortune 500, midsize, and small corporations. In DevOps, the traditional separation of software development and the server administration and infrastructure support groups is dissolved into a single unit. In the past, waterfall software development in a corporation would begin with developing and releasing a service or program without sufficient testing or documentation, with the expectation that the corporation's operations would support and maintain the new software. This caused conflict, crashed systems, and angered end users because the software was not sufficiently tested under "real-world" conditions. Software bugs and problems that were not being adequately addressed in software development became the responsibility of the system and hardware

Becoming a Lean Library
ISBN 978-1-84334-779-8

maintenance team as the original developers shifted to new projects or left the corporation. As is often the case, the end users typically figured modifications or other maneuvers to compensate for the bugs and lacking functionality in the software.

Combining these two functions within the same divisional or organizational structure comes from upper management's realization that internal IT and software development provides to the company a critical competitive advantage in the marketplace. Even for corporations or organizations that are not remotely associated with software development, institutions use a mixture of software products, along with sometimes extensive customization, to give decision makers critical information about current operations and predictive statistics and reports about their industry's competitive environment and markets. Referring back to Boyd's OODA loop, these internally developed applications give organizations and corporations the communication and analysis tools for iterating faster through the orient and decide phases of the loop.

Shortening project lead times and blurring between customer, fan, and support staff are all forcing the internal IT departments in many corporations to be nimble and responsive to changing requirements while improving the reliability and functionality of their products and services. In adopting more agile and lean startup ideas and techniques by a new combined DevOps unit, organizations are starting to better meet these new challenges and opportunities. Libraries—larger academic and public libraries in particular—resemble, both in function and in the delivery of services, the type of midsize corporation that is a typical adopter of DevOps.

DevOps complements another trend in corporate information—that of shifting corporate information infrastructure and resources from being managed and controlled locally in large data centers to using cloud computing providers for either fully hosted applications and hardware stacks or, in a more common model, that of using a hybrid mixture of internally supported infrastructure and external, third-party cloud hosting. This mixture offers a much more flexible and lean infrastructure that can expand or contract depending on the requirements and demands of the corporate end users and customers. Development of new services or expansion and refactoring of existing applications can now be better provisioned with computing resources from cloud-hosting companies. Instead of the IT department trying to forecast the technology demands of its users months or even years ahead, IT resources in a DevOps unit are allocated and delivered by the pull of demand from the end users. Major library systems are shifting to more cloud-based delivery systems with the Online Computer Library Center's WorldCat, Ex Libris Alma, or Ebsco Discovery Services, which are wholly or partially available on public or private cloud environments; other vendors, like III, now offer fully hosted variants of their respective systems.

Even though DevOps is closely linked with cloud-based computing, the exciting possibilities of providing even better technology services that utilize all of the talents and experience of staff goes beyond the enabling technology of cloud computing. DevOps provides the organizational "glue" for building and supporting these new technologies in lean libraries.

9.1 CHARACTERISTICS OF A HEALTHY DEVOPS DEPARTMENT

Like other models for software development and operations, corporations and organizations have varying degrees of success in implementing or adopting a DevOps structure for their IT departments. Most of these characteristics are shared by successful lean startups and lean manufacturers and provide a promising model for libraries.

- **Short, iterative development cycles**: DevOps allows an organization to experiment with and release new products and services faster through a build–measure–learn cycles, starting with minimal viable products (MVPs) that run on the production infrastructure. Having the end users—even if those users are internal to the organization—use and test the actual product that will eventually be released by the DevOps group means problems are noticed sooner and fixed faster.

- **Driven by Metrics**: For more strategic or long-term development efforts, requirements for a new or upgraded product or service start out as ambiguous and unclear. Using lean startup methodologies, testable hypotheses, and the development of MVPs gives immediate feedback to the developers and supporters of the product or service, providing decision makers with valuable information about the continued viability of the current process. If a pivot is needed to better align the project with the operational and strategic goals of the organization, the metrics provide support for that decision.

- **Focused on People**: A library's DevOps department, even in library systems with a single member, must always focus on the people being served. A library patron is usually and properly the focus for most libraries. An important cohort for library DevOps is other departments and services internal to the library or the library's partners in a consortium. Following a pull strategy, communication between the patrons should drive the research and implementation of any new technology or enhancements to existing products and/or services.

The library's technical services and systems groups need to drive analysis and decision making based on the actual usage of the library system's patrons and the vision of library leadership to seek out the edges in their communities. Meeting these challenges requires much adjustment and retooling, comparable to what many large manufactures are doing to reorganize their operations to become more lean. Moving from disconnected to connected, from an isolated to a valued participant in the emerging Linked Data and semantic Web worlds, should mean that libraries are natural fits for their communities' emerging information needs.

Libraries—public libraries in particular—have been seen primarily as institutions for collecting and sharing resources, but a shift is occurring whereby this view is being expanded such that the library is a now center for creation. By building on and expanding libraries' existing efforts to offer more creation space for different cohorts of patrons, through makerspaces, digital laboratories with higher-end audio and video editing hardware and software, and even craft areas for children and young adults, libraries are active in the production of cultural, scholarly, or entertainment artifacts within their communities. To better support these activities and meet these challenges, which often have extensive technology requirements, libraries can implement DevOps and lean organizational principles. The core idea is to let the demand for technology and related services by the libraries' communities drive the provision and implementation of IT resources.

9.2 DEVOPS FOR LARGER ORGANIZATIONS

DevOps is viable only if a library's leadership recognizes that the library's technology-based resources and services should be lean and more responsive in meeting patrons and staff needs. This may be difficult for library leadership to consider if there exists misunderstanding or even active hostility between various departments in the library. Entrenched positions, with departments defining and defending their "turf" within the library, occurs more often than library leadership may want to admit. Even within the library's systems and technical services departments, fractures can exist between different individuals or groups responsible for specific technology services.

For libraries with large IT organizations, many of the characteristics and processes of DevOps can be used to restructure the development, operations, and quality control functions of the library's technical services and systems operations. Within these larger organizations, the interdependence of developing software, rigorous testing for quality assurance, deploying the entire application in a production environment, and then subsequently maintaining the software application can be integrated by deliberately merging these different functions into a single department. The entire life cycle of the application in production may be better managed through the appointment of a release coordinator. The release coordinator uses a diverse set of tools, such as project management software, wikis, and spreadsheets, to shepherd through the deployments of the software application, from initial development and quality assurance testing to maintenance inside and outside the library.

In larger libraries that are sponsors for open-source projects, the release coordinator manages the development and testing of software applications by other libraries and organizations. The release coordinator ensures that new changes are successfully deployed within the library's IT infrastructure. These diverse team members, perhaps globally distributed, may require extensive coordination with the library's internal systems. The release coordinator communicates the development status of the application between the development team and the systems operators or administrators. The release coordinator should be familiar with the complex infrastructure of their individual library and also have a passing familiarity with the other institutions' IT infrastructures as the software application is developed among the partners in the project.

DevOps applied to IT organizations in large libraries must still support existing software and services. These software services include e-mail, calendars, content management, enterprise resource management, accounting, student management, and learning systems. For these established services, a DevOps lean library should not unnecessarily change existing services, especially when starting to adopt a DevOps model. Legacy software should be changed or modified only if the demands for the services change or if the costs for support drastically increase. Other reasons for changing legacy software is if a significantly better product is released or if the hidden costs of support start to outweigh the benefits. Legacy software within a library's technology infrastructure still benefit from adopting DevOps. New modifications or customizations are now more rigorously tracked and tested before being released to the end users. A DevOps

environment also allows for more creative ways to meet library requirements than legacy software, including shifting hosting and maintenance to
a service provider that runs on external computing resources outside the
library's both public and private clouds.

Implementing DevOps can be difficult, however, especially with
entrenched practices and myopic staff who are unduly committed to their
particular job function and skill set. A library with DevOps and, more
broadly, lean organizational principles devotes more resources to training and
coaching its employees about new models, workflows, and technological
processes. To fully embrace lean ideas requires a shift in library leadership's
thinking, coupled with empowering all library staff to become more auton-
omous. Employees should be responsible for learning new skills, discovering
new ideas, and offering innovative improvements to existing workflows.

9.3 DEVOPS FOR SMALLER LIBRARIES

For smaller libraries with few or no IT staff, many DevOps practices and
processes may not be applicable when there are only a few individuals with
responsibilities that cover multiple domains. The individual who develops
or implements a library-specific customization often is also responsible for
quality assurance testing and deploying the customization in the library's
production environment. However, the technology and processes of
DevOps have value even to these small libraries with limited resources and
personnel.

The DevOps movement has seen the rise of technology and processes for
automating the development and deployment of server or cloud technologies using configuration management tools such as Docker, Chief, Saltstack,
Ansible, and Puppet. These tools help to ensure that the software environment that the application is developed under can be replicated in the library's
production environment. While most libraries do not have a dedicated data
center for their technology, knowing at least some of the details of the larger
IT infrastructure that the library is part of can be critical for troubleshooting
and deploying the software application. Individuals external to the library's IT
(and who are not usually directly employed by the library) should be included
in library meetings and process so that they can learn the requirements and
other dependencies of library-specific software applications. These external
IT representatives can then forward the library-specific applications to the
appropriate group responsible for operating and deploying the application to
the library's users.

Small libraries, particularly rural libraries or academic libraries at smaller colleges or universities, often depend on a third party, such as a library consortium or their campus IT departments. A library interested in using lean processes to improve their patron-focused resources and services should encourage the formation of ad hoc project teams that include librarians and/or staff, consortium partners, and any external IT contacts into lateral-based groups. With such teams it may be more difficult to coordinate quick iterations of a build–measure–learn loop for an MVP; however, by reducing the scope of the MVP and extending the duration of each iteration, the team can still realize benefits of a lean development and release process. Communication and coordination become even more important in such situations (both of these activities are critical to any size organization implementing lean processes), where individuals can be both geographically dispersed coupled with operating under different management and organizational structures.

It may take a concerted effort to create agreement and support for the successful deployment of a software product produced through the DevOps partnerships established by a library. Small libraries functioning as a learning organization for members of their communities should be able to start responding to and building the library as a creation hub for its community; this is a feature of DevOps. Small libraries should be encouraged to concentrate and develop the unique and specific interests of their communities by building lean organizations supported by open and transparent pull systems. Using a DevOps approach within a larger lean organizational philosophy, small libraries transform themselves into learning and empowered memory organizations that are vital to their communities.

9.4 CATALOG PULL PLATFORM CASE STUDY: SUPPORTING DEVOPS AT THE TUTT LIBRARY

The systems group at the Tutt Library at Colorado College has only two members, Jon Driscoll and Jeremy Nelson. Jeremy Nelson handles development, while Jon handles operations. Each of them has a different set of responsibilities with different requirements for the Catalog Pull Platform.

Because of the small size of the systems department at Tutt Library, automation tools such as Fabric and Grunt, along with the virtual machine manager Docker, are used to simplify and automate the various components of the Catalog Pull Platform, as well as the systems and its predecessor programs, such as the legacy Aristotle Discovery Layer and a handful of HTML5 applications in the Aristotle Library Apps and the Colorado College Electronic Thesis projects.

The Tutt Library systems group is dependent on the Colorado College's IT group for network infrastructure, virtual machines, and other technology services that cannot reasonably be handled by the systems group. In 2013 the library's legacy integrated library system was moved from being hosted on a dedicated server in the library's basement to a version that is hosted at the vendor's data center in California. Other library services that are not hosted in the library include the library's digital repository, which is hosted by a regional consortium, the Colorado Association of Research Libraries, as well as other services offered by the consortium, including Prospector, a union catalog, and RAPID for interlibrary loan fulfillment of journal articles.

CHAPTER 10

The Future as a Warehouse

"Open," a concept capacious enough to contain both the communal and capitalistic impulses central to Web 2.0 while being thankfully free of any socialist connotations.

Taylor (2004)

10.1 RECLAIMING "BOOK WAREHOUSE"

When libraries are referred to derisively as just "book warehouses," instead of ducking away or changing the subject, they should embrace that categorization. Many of the most successful corporations developed their competitive advantage because their highly automated and efficient warehouse operations. Amazon fulfills millions of orders with few staff because of their ability to store and retrieve of a wide range of consumer goods beyond books. Wal-Mart is able to out-compete their competition in part because of its ability to efficiently manage and deliver its inventory to thousands of stores through a pull system that connects to large warehouses (Traub, 2012). FedEx uses a central hubs that are similar to Amazon's and Wal-Mart's warehouses to efficiently route their packages throughout the United States and the world.

Even though libraries as warehouses is cliche, this "straw man" argument falters under closer scrutiny. In the foreword to a 1965 history of the Detroit Library, Ralph Shaw wrote, "The Detroit Public Library picked up the thread of history just as our nation was moving from the concept of libraries as storehouses of books—considered as precious physical objects for the use of the few—to the conception of books and libraries as people" (Woodford, 1965). Although thoughtful writers and thinkers have rejected the characterization of a library as a warehouse of dead books, this does not mean that libraries need to reject such categorization as well.

Popular visualizations of a warehouse are often like a Dickensian caricature of a nineteenth- or early twentieth-century sweatshop. Employees work in dirty and dangerous conditions while trying to organize and navigate a complex maze of shelving while being constantly watched and critiqued by impersonal managers. Finding any one specific item is difficult, if not impossible, with large inventories being stored with minimal

Becoming a Lean Library
ISBN 978-1-84334-779-8

documentation. While the reality of the twenty-first-century warehouse is usually different (although Amazon has been criticized for the low pay and long hours in their warehouses, leading to reports of mental illness among employees [BBC, 2013]), modern warehouse operations are usually highly automated and supported by a large information technology infrastructure.

In the adoption of inventory management technologies such as radiofrequency identification (RFID) and visual bar codes, coupled with more and more collections being moved to online, libraries are starting to resemble their commercial counterparts. Libraries emphasize how their space and collections are part of a larger movement away from being just warehouses of books (as if libraries have always been just about their books). Libraries embrace a future of collaborative creation spaces supported by an increasingly diverse collection of materials.

Libraries' collections of knowledge stocks comprise discrete artifacts and the information infrastructure surrounding the access and management of those artifacts. Enabling varied and different types of knowledge flows among the local communities libraries serve means connecting them to other individuals and interests ranging across the globe. Librarians worry about and plan for the use of an institution's physical space, as they continue in their efforts to encourage the creation of, and then explicitly capture, the knowledge flows that occur among and within the library's communities of patrons, staff, and librarians. The fuzzy boundaries between a knowledge stock and a knowledge flow allow libraries to extend and embrace their role as warehouses. How long material is stored and actively curated as geographic or subject collections at memory institutions, and as those collections are transformed into more active knowledge flows, libraries' resemblance to the modern automated warehouse becomes both more obvious in one perspective but very different when considered from others.

10.2 SMART COLLECTIONS

The hype cycle is building on what Bruce Sterling (2004) coined as "spimes," or the "Internet of Things,"—that is, smart objects that trace, record, and compute through embedded and networked presences. A first step toward smart collections is adding RFID chips to physical objects in the library. RFID chips are small, printed circuits that are permanently attached to an item; there typically are two types: active and passive. Active RFID is more expensive because the chips broadcast information to a receiver, whereas with passive RFID, the chip transmits its identification when scanned by a receiver. Most libraries that implement RFID use the passive model because of the expense and because the broadcast feature of active RFID is not necessary for inventory and management of a library's physical material collections. Passive RFID is typically the technology behind self-service kiosks seen in more modern libraries that have such services for their patrons.

Libraries that use RFID technology as a circulation and inventory tool for their collections have the potential to expand the service and usability of their collections. By attaching RFID tags to items, libraries are in the beginning stages of a more augmented and embedded library. While the library does not typically capture much provenance or origin information of a book beyond such information as producer, publisher, or distributor, the decreasing cost in computer storage, along with the more sophisticated software and tools in the supply chains of larger, typically commercial man-ufacturing and distribution companies, means that more information can be captured and associated with the book throughout its creation and life within the library. Any book in the library can now be tracked throughout its life span, along with its provenance and reader annotations. Another possible outcome of adopting RFID is that a library can be participant in the afterlife of a book as it is weeded and removed from the library's collection. It would be hard to justify the additional expense of providing an item's rich history after it is no longer owned or managed by the library, but such data may become more valuable as the history of an item is tracked. The library may be able to offer such "postlibrary" data services through a public application program interface.

Even the addition of this deacquisition cost when a library discards an item should not be missed as an opportunity to extend the library's services regarding the provenance of the item. The difference between the physical and digital is just a temporary condition; this descriptive extension of even the most mundane object will reflect positively on libraries in the future.

10.3 PEER-TO-PEER LENDING

The addition of more detailed tracking of physical items with RFID in libraries also opens new opportunities for libraries to coordinate the transfer of resources between patrons. For example, with the implementation of newer services it is now possible for a patron to lend library material to another person without first returning the book or item to the library. Going even further, the library can coordinate the pickup of material through the postal service and its delivery to another patron without the need for the patron to return the item to the library first and the library then hold the item for another patron. This coordination of material outside the library is possible with current library technology, it but would require much manual intervention by library staff. As libraries and their collections become more integrated with their communities, the line between the library holding an item and the item's actual location—either on the library's shelves or in a patron's possession—because blurred.

In the Catalog Pull Platform, a conscious decision was made to allow the catalog itself to change and adapt to the needs and usage of the patrons and institutions. In the first iterations, patrons were encouraged to view the machine-readable catalog, BIBFRAME, and schema.org visualizations of various works and choose those properties that should be displayed to the patrons accessing the catalog. These cultural artifacts now become part of the transactional and narrative elements of the spime by taking a statistical snapshot of patrons' personal views and then displaying the most popular information to the casual users of the catalog. Future iterations of the Catalog Pull Platform will examine whether RFID and item bar codes could create coordinated services so that students in the same class could lend books to each other without the need to have the item physical pass through the library's circulation department.

10.4 EXTENDING INTO COMMUNITIES

Why should a future as a warehouse extend and enhance a library in local, regional, national, and global communities? A library's collections soon will extend even farther beyond its walls, beyond the scope of its patrons, its staff, and its local communities. Smart collections with engaged and responsive masters of the knowledge flows—known as librarians—extend through and into library patrons' lives. Libraries of all types currently strive to be responsive to their communities, but the mechanism and process for doing so can be ad hoc and reactive. This book has described different lean approaches, techniques, and ways in which libraries can be more intentional in their planning and delivery of resources and services as the information and service needs of their communities change over time. As libraries expand their collecting efforts with different types and volumes of increasingly digital and hybrid artifacts created in their communities, they become even more integrated with the creative forces and knowledge flows within their patrons' lives.

Libraries functioning as publishers do not necessarily need to provide all of the services of a traditional publisher, including copyediting, marketing, printing, and distributing, but they should offer a platform that allows works to be preserved and hosted, along with the ability for readers and consumers to augment and annotate the resource over time. As traditional publishers evolve, they may start offering their services in a more granular fashion, offering each of these services as separate functions that a library could then pick and choose to offer in their services as a local publisher in their communities.

Sharing resources between libraries and various organizations becomes easier with the evolution of smart collections. Libraries function both as amplifiers and filters, attracting the kind of serendipitous encounters between their collections and their patrons that are the mutually beneficial to both the patron and the library. A point that needs to be repeated is that these encounters between a library's patrons, its staff, and its collections are reciprocal relationships.

Projects that flow through a lean library should change and morph after multiple and varied build–measure–learn iterations; libraries can capturing a project's metadata and creative outputs in each build–measure–learn iteration, promoting learning over time. This ability to capture a project's narrative can also be applied to other creative narratives that emerge from successful and even unsuccessful book, film, music, gaming, and software development, and other group-based efforts that end with new artifacts. These creative efforts generate digital ephemera from project management, promotion, and delivery avenues for the published creative work, and libraries can now shift into new roles in capturing and preserving these additional artifacts.

10.5 INCREASING SERENDIPITY THROUGH CREATION SPACES

As learning organizations firmly attached to particular physical locations, libraries have places for encountering new ideas and new possibilities. Discoveries made while using a library while browsing the stacks are a strong and romantic reason to keep books in libraries, but this is, surprisingly, a recent sentiment that is only as old as World War II (Barclay, 2010). In the new information-rich environment, where individuals access so much more information through search engines and social networks, the value and opportunity for serendipitous encounters may be decreased. To promote the awareness and value of getting individuals in the community to share their often rich stores of tacit knowledge, libraries need to be more explicit about the value of serendipitous encounters between their patrons and their librarians and staff. Libraries aspire to be neutral and safe places for individuals who have rich stores of knowledge, particularly about local geography and history, that offer the library new and expanded opportunities to warehouse these valuable intellectual assets.

Those events that cannot be forecast or predicted, while not usually a written as tracked outcomes, are important elements of a well-functioning lean library. Attempts to shape these random encounters occur through optimizing the chances for members of the library's communities to encounter each other, whether physically in the library or online. Can a library increase the scope and number of serendipitous encounters between patrons and staff, encouraging face-to-face interaction while balancing both the time and energy needed to make each encounter productive for both the staff member and the patron?

The following is an example of how a library provides an environment for serendipitous encounters, when the author was a graduate assistant at the University of Illinois commerce library and working on the reference desk, an alumnus of the university stopped by on a Saturday afternoon. The alumnus related how, approximately 10 years earlier, he had been browsing the popular magazines at the library and came across an idea that he later turned into a successful business. The patron now visited libraries looking for new and unexpected opportunities for his next venture. A library's environment may not necessarily inspire entirely new businesses, but the physical structures and supportive staff should be conductive to increasing the opportunities for the library's patrons to engage and interact with its collections, as well as with its inspired and thoughtful staff.

As public institutions, libraries already offer environments that encourage serendipitous encounters. Even the physical layout of a library's collections—where, for the most part, material is organized by call number or by topic—means that patrons with similar reading tastes or patterns will be physically co-located when browsing for books. Libraries, particularly K–12 and public libraries, are also shifting from being just the physical location of physical collections to including cooperative spaces intended for the patrons and staff to encourage creation of the new and the remixing of the existing resources of the library. Such spaces, whether they are new three-dimensional makerspaces, digital labs, or a dedicated arts and crafts area, are already being explored by libraries as the demands for these types of creation spaces by their communities increase. Libraries have always been places for sharing ideas and creation; the difference now is that libraries are being more deliberate and intentional about planning and supporting the repurposing of the physical space in the library.

Some library practices also encourage serendipitous encounters among the library's patrons and staff. The availability of trained reference librarians, whether at a separate service point in the library or combined with a circulation service point, is one example. A reference librarian increases serendipitous encounters among patrons not only by giving a patron pointers on how to structure a research query but also by redirecting the patron to other, more specialized services within the library. Although the tradition of keeping the reference center in a central location is the dominant model for reference services in libraries, expanding and reinterpreting this role to being more of a facilitator and creator of serendipitous events could mean that librarians are more mobile, actively assisting patrons searching for physical items in the collections or becoming embedded in the work being done by the community.

As the authors of *The Power of Pull* note in the chapter on attracting and increasing the opportunities for serendipitous encounters, professional conferences "become important gathering spots on emerging edges where people perceive an urgent need to come together with others to share experiences and connect, jointly addressing the challenges and opportunities arising on the edge" (Hagel III, Brown, & Davison, 2010, p. 103). In addition to sending staff to professional conferences, a library can create local environments that replicate many of the advantages of professional conferences by holding workshops, seminars, and even small conferences on topics of interest to the communities they serve. By being a known location for gatherings, libraries not only give their patrons the advantages of creating connections among themselves, these more formal meetings offer opportunities for libraries to build services and resources that serve these interested and engaged groups in their communities.

Finally, a library, whether the staff or the patrons, can increase its preparedness for a serendipitous encounter that occurs within the library. Libraries can promote, plan, and schedule space with different physical infrastructures and characteristics to support serendipitous encounters between individuals in the community. The marketing and promotion capabilities that a library can offer to creators also draws together like-minded individuals who may not be aware that others share their particular passion or interest. Libraries' promotion of creative spaces should not be restricted to their Web site, newsletter, or e-mail distribution lists, but should extend into the various social networks of their creator communities.

10.6 LEADING FROM THE EDGE

Reflecting the massive changes that are occurring in the larger society, libraries adapt and change in an environment of increasingly shorter attention spans among their patrons. The peripheries, or edges, in libraries and technologies in related fields may be where innovations that libraries should consider adopting are happening. What and where are these related fields? It is hoped that this book provides ideas and lessons from lean startup and lean manufacturing that can assist libraries in supporting and creating resources and services for their various communities.

Lean libraries function as laboratories for exploring and creating environments, attitudes, and cultures that foster the creative spectrum of their served communities. Capturing and sharing of libraries should be encouraged through an expanded definition of what their collections and physical spaces are. As more material becomes available online, the role of librarians as guides, mentors, and coaches within this complex informational environment becomes even important.

The Learner and Leadership Badge communities that have been actively developed around *Becoming a Lean Library* are about extending the ideas of a lean library to people in the library profession and beyond. The ideas behind lean organizations and pull platforms for libraries require that libraries and memory institution have mechanisms in place for encouraging participants to connect with each other. The online home for the *Becoming a Lean Library* sends e-mails or text messages when a badge earners post items related to their interactions with other badge participants. Fully honoring the privacy of badge earners, rich integration possibilities also exist for reader participation in LinkedIn, Facebook, Pinterest, Tumblr, and Twitter social networks.

The nexus in this network is the book's Web site, which coordinates and extends knowledge flows from a principal hub out to the open Web and reader communities. Ingesting and integrating incoming knowledge flows is easy. For example, the author's tweets about a topic or announcement related to the book, including the hash tag #lean-libraries, are collected, streamed, and saved as annotations to sections on the book's Web site. These book and community annotations are managed by a semantic server from the Catalog Pull Platform that can then be linked directly into the badge participants' professional and formal educational processes and reviews.

How can libraries and librarians find new ways of pulling people who operate on the edges, and their knowledge, into productive dialogues? The dialogue between library staff and patrons, as well as the dialogue among library staff, encourage and increase the dialogue among the communities that make up a library's patrons. Libraries shift and become known as unique warehouses of ideas and creative works, where serendipity and knowledge flow naturally from the library's environment of engaged people in a lean learning organization.

The value of libraries in the twenty-first century will increasingly come from their intangible assets—the knowledge and reputation of their librarians and staff, their services and outreach—and less from considering libraries as the gatekeepers to a published corpus of printed material. Libr[THIS LINE]ies' collections are now broader and narrower than in previous generations, and the new role of librarians, as one of many sources of pull, is to become more involved with the intangible needs of individuals. Greater cross-collaboration among libraries—not just among similar types of libraries (e.g., public to public and academic to academic) but across different types of libraries (e.g., public to academic, K-12 to public, and academic to special)—offers new ways that the edges of libraries offer leadership and service to all of the communities being served.

This seems to be what is considered local and global blurs; actually, for libraries, this may have always been the case. Leading from the edge also means a need to shift libraries toward becoming creation spaces that are not just restricted to being repositories for preexisting explicit knowledge stocks but instead bring the creativity of the global community into the lives of the individual patrons and libraries' present and future communities.

REFERENCES

Adler, P. (1998). *Building better bureaucracies*. Retrieved from http://ceo.usc.edu/pdf/G98303 58.pdf.

ALA. (2014). *Code of Ethics of the American Library Association*. Retrieved from http://www.ala.org/advocacy/proethics/codeofethics/codeethics.

Anderson, C. (2005). Long tail. *Wired, 12. 10.* Retrieved from http://archive.wired.com/wired/archive/12.10/tail.html.

Anderson, C. (2006). *The long tail*. New York, NY: Hyperion.

Anderson, R. (2013). Confronting the problem of surplus value. *Library Journal*. Retrieved from http://lj.libraryjournal.com/2013/05/opinion/peer-to-peer-review/confronting-the-problem-of-surplus-value/.

Barclay, D. (2010). Academic library space in the age of Facebook. *American Libraries*. Retrieved from http://www.americanlibrariesmagazine.org/article/myth-browsing.

BBC. (2013). *Amazon workers face 'increased risk of mental illness'*. Retrieved from http://www.bbc.com/news/business-25034598.

Bernes Lee, T. (1992). *Cool URIs don't change*. Retrieved from http://www.w3.org/Provider/Style/URI.html.

Blank, S. (2012). *Why the lean start-up changes everything*.

Breeding, M. (2013). Automation Marketplace 2013: The rush to innovate. *Library Journal*. Retrieved from http://www.thedigitalshift.com/2013/04/ils/automation-marketplace-2013-the-rush-to-innovate/.

Breeding, M. (2014). Library systems report 2014: Competition and strategic cooperation. *American Libraries Magazine*. Retrieved from http://americanlibrariesmagazine.org/2014/04/15/library-systems-report-2014/.

Cafezeiro, I., & Haeusler, E. (2007). Semantic interoperability via category theory. In *Proceeding ER '07 tutorials, posters, panels, and industrial contributions at the 26th international conference on conceptual modeling* (83). Retrieved from http://crpit.com/confpapers/CRPITV 83Cafezeiro.pdf.

Dempsey, L. (2006). *Libraries and the long tail*. Retrieved from http://www.dlib.org/dlib/april06/dempsey/04dempsey.html.

Dougherty, R., & Heinritz, F. (1966). *Scientific management of library operations*. New York, NY: Scarecrow Press.

Godin, S. (2011). *The future of the library: What is a public library for*. Retrieved from http://sethgodin.typepad.com/seths_blog/2011/05/the-future-of-the-library.html.

Hagel, J., III, Brown, J., & Davison, L. (2010). *The power of pull: How small moves smartly made, can set big things in motion*. New York, NY: Basic Books.

Hagell, J., III, Brown, J. S., & Kulasooriya, D. (2011). *The 2011 shift index: Measuring the forces of long-term change*. Retrieved from http://www2.deloitte.com/content/dam/Deloitte/nl/Documents/center-for-the-edge/deloitte-nl-center-for-the-edge-shift-index.pdf.

Haibel, B. (2014). The fantasy and abuse of the manipulable user. *Model View Culture*. Retrieved from http://modelviewculture.com/pieces/the-fantasy-and-abuse-of-the-manipulable-user.

Hildreth, C. (1995). *Online Catalog Design Models: Are We Moving in the Right Direction?* Retrieved from http://myweb.cwpost.liu.edu/childret/clr-opac.html.

Kopp, R. (2010). *Hansei - Apologizing Japanese Style*. Retrieved from http://www.japaninterc ultural.com/en/news/default.aspx?newsID=52.

Lamont, M. (2009). Gender, Technology, and Libraries. *Information Technology and Libraries*, *28*(3). Retrieved from http://ejournals.bc.edu/ojs/index.php/ital/article/view/3221/2834.

Liker, J. (2004). *The Toyota way*. New York, NY: McGraw-Hill.

Lyle, D. (2011). *Goodbye, OODA Loop*. Retrieved from http://www.armedforcesjournal.com/goodbye-ooda-loop/.

Madison, I. (2012). Ivory Madison. In *Lean startup conference 2012*. Retrieved from https://www.youtube.com/watch?v=l2z9zb1W72Y.

Maurya, A. (2012). *Why Lean Canvas vs Business Model Canvas?* Retrieved from http://leanstack.com/why-lean-canvas/.

Pessach, G. (2000). [Networked] memory institutions: social remembering, privatization, and its discontents. *Cardozo Arts & Entertainment Law Journal*. Retrieved from http://papers.ssrn.com/sol3/papers.cfm?abstract_id=1085267.

Poole, N. (2014). *Make it personal–Designing services that people will love*. Keynote presentation at ILMS Webwise conference. Retrieved from http://www.collectionstrust.org.uk/blog/past-posts/item/13496-anchoring-communities-keynote-to-ilms-webwise-2014.

Ries, E. (2011). *The lean startup*. New York, NY: Crown Business.

Salo, D. (2010). *Retooling Libraries for the Data Challenge*. Ariadne. 64.

Schmidt, A. (2013). *Focus on people, not tools*. Retrieved from http://www.walkingpaper.org/6000.

Schonfeld, R. (2013). *Stop the presses: Is the monograph headed toward an e-only future?* Retrieved from http://www.sr.ithaka.org/blog-individual/stop-presses-monograph-headed-toward-e-only-future.

Spivak, D. (2013). *Category theory for scientists*. Retrieved from: http://math.mit.edu/~dspivak/CT4S.pdf.

Sterling, B. (2004). *When bioobjects rule the earth*. Retrieved from http://www.viridiandesign.org/notes/401-450/00422_the_spime.html.

Sternstein, A. (2005). Librarians face existential crisis. *FCW*. Retrieved from http://fcw.com/articles/2005/04/15/librarians-face-existential-crisis.aspx.

Taylor, A. (2014). *The people's platform*. pp. 123–125, 127.

Torkington, N. (2011). *Libraries: Where it all went wrong*. Retrieved from http://nathan.torkington.com/blog/2011/11/23/libraries-where-it-all-went-wrong/.

Traub, T. (2012). Wal-Mart used technology to become supply chain leader. *Arkansas Business*. Retrieved from http://www.arkansasbusiness.com/article/85508/wal-mart-used-technology-to-become-supply-chain-leader?page=all.

Verborgh, R. (2013). *The Lie of the API*. Retrieved from http://ruben.verborgh.org/blog/2013/11/29/the-lie-of-the-api/.

Welker, J. (2012). Counting on COUNTER: the current state of e-resource usage data in libraries. *Computers in Libraries*. Retrieved from http://www.infotoday.com/cilmag/nov12/Welker–Counting-on-COUNTER.shtml.

Williams, M. (2011). *Ebooks and the existential crisis of libraries*. Retrieved from http://librarian.newjackalmanac.ca/2011/03/ebooks-and-existential-crises-of.html.

Womack, J., & Jones, D. (2003). *Lean Thinking: Banish Waste and Create Wealth in Your Corporation, Revised and Updated*. New York, NY: Productivity Press.

Woodford, F. (1965). *Parnassus on main street*. Detroit, MI: Wayne State University Press.

Zickur, k., Rainie, L., Purcell, k. (2013). *How Americans Value Their Communities*. Washington, DC: Pew Research Center. Retrieved from http://libraries.pewinternet.org/2013/12/11/libraries-in-communities/.

INDEX

Note: Page numbers followed by "f" and "t" indicate figures and tables, respectively.

Printed in the United States
By Bookmasters